Where Is the Promise of His Coming?

Where Is the Promise of His Coming?

The Delay of the Parousia in the New Testament

DAVID L. MATHEWSON

CASCADE Books • Eugene, Oregon

WHERE IS THE PROMISE OF HIS COMING?
The Delay of the Parousia in the New Testament

Copyright © 2018 David L. Mathewson. All rights reserved. Except for brief quotations in critical publications or reviews, no part of this book may be reproduced in any manner without prior written permission from the publisher. Write: Permissions, Wipf and Stock Publishers, 199 W. 8th Ave., Suite 3, Eugene, OR 97401.

Cascade Books
An Imprint of Wipf and Stock Publishers
199 W. 8th Ave., Suite 3
Eugene, OR 97401

www.wipfandstock.com

PAPERBACK ISBN: 978-1-5326-1649-5
HARDCOVER ISBN: 978-1-5326-1649-5
EBOOK ISBN: 978-1-5326-7004-6

Cataloging-in-Publication data:

Names: Mathewson, David, author.

Title: Where is the promise of his coming? : the delay of the parousia in the New Testament / David L. Mathewson.

Description: Eugene, OR : Cascade Books, 2018 | Includes bibliographical references and index.

Identifiers: ISBN 978-1-5326-1649-5 (paperback) | ISBN 978-1-5326-1649-5 (hardcover) | ISBN 978-1-5326-7004-6 (ebook)

Subjects: LCSH: Eschatology—Biblical teaching. | Second Advent—Biblical teaching. | Theology, Doctrinal. | Eschatology.

Classification: LCC BT821.3 M383 2018 (print) | LCC BT821.3 (ebook)

Manufactured in the U.S.A.   10/25/18

Contents

Acknowledgments | vii

1 Introduction: Where Is the Promise of His Coming? | 1
2 The Gospels | 13
3 Acts and Paul's Letters | 38
4 The General Epistles | 61
5 Revelation | 74
6 Conclusion: Where Is the Promise of His Coming? | 97

Bibliography | 113
Scripture Index | 117

Acknowledgments

I have spent most of my academic career thinking about and writing about eschatology in some form. However, almost all of my thinking and writing on this topic has been for academic purposes (books, article, academic presentations), with little aimed directly at the church. It has always been my practice, however, to take what I do in my academic study and make it relevant to the church, the people of God, not just to the academic guild. Therefore, I am delighted to devote a book on a specific topic of eschatology to the broader audience of the church. I pray that my thinking of the topic of how we handle the issue of the delay of Christ's coming will prove helpful to the readers of this book. I hope that this work will help God's people think sensibly about eschatology. But more specifically, I hope that this book will inspire confidence in the hope that we have of the sure and soon return of Jesus Christ at his second coming. And I hope that its readers will be challenged to live responsibly and with a sense of urgency in light of the certainty of Christ's coming.

I would like to thank several people whom I highly respect and admire, and whose opinions I greatly value for reading parts of this book and offering valuable feedback that has made its way into this book. Thank you Craig L. Blomberg, Caleb Mathewson, Steve Mathewson, and Shari Simmons for taking the time to read sections of my book and for making it a better work with your suggestions and encouragement.

1

Introduction
Where Is the Promise of His Coming?

INTRODUCTION

The church has always confessed that one day Christ will return to earth to bring history to its goal and to set up his kingdom on earth. This hope formed part of the early Christian creeds and continues to feature in modern-day church confessional statements. The expectation of the return of Christ finds support in nearly every book of the New Testament (see below) and is anticipated in the pages of the Old Testament. The promise of Christ's return has led also to numerous attempts throughout church history to calculate more or less precisely the time when the return of Christ to earth as promised in the New Testament will happen. Usually, major political shifts, technological or scientific discoveries, or cosmic disruptions and natural disasters serve to spark new predictions that the end must be near. Christians, some well-meaning, have appealed to such signs as these to determine how "soon" Christ's coming might be. Surely we are the privileged generation that will see the long-awaited return of Christ to earth. But all such attempts to predict the timing of Christ's return have had one thing in common: to date they have all failed miserably! So time marches on, and two thousand years after the last New

Where Is the Promise of His Coming?

Testament writer (John and the book of Revelation) assured readers that Christ would come back, and soon (22:20), Christ still has not returned.

This tension of waiting for an end that never comes ends up evoking a variety of responses from those within our churches. Some respond by ignoring the problem and just cling to the hope that Christ will still come back, while in the meantime distracting themselves with other things (witnessing or ministry of some type). Often this is accompanied with the passing word of assurance that everything will "pan out" in the end. Some will continue to jump on the bandwagon of every new prediction that we are living in the last generation and will see the Lord's return in our lifetime. Such teachings are always popular, despite of the long history of failed predictions. For others, the tension leads to a crisis of faith and perhaps even the eventual abandonment of their Christian belief. If the Bible got it wrong on this fundamental issue, surely there is no reason to trust it on anything else! Interestingly, this "crisis" seems to be precipitated by statements by the biblical authors themselves. After all, did not even the New Testament authors, and Jesus himself, in the first century say that Christ would come back *soon* or that his coming was *near*?

At the heart of Jesus' teaching in the Gospels was the announcement of the arrival of the long-awaited kingdom of God promised in the Old Testament prophets.[1] The first three Evangelists (Matthew, Mark, and Luke) all agree on this characteristic feature of Jesus' preaching at the outset of his adult earthly ministry: "'The time has come,' he said. 'The kingdom of God has come near. Repent and believe the good news!'"[2] (Mark 1:15; see Matt 4:17; Luke 4:43). Apparently, with the coming of Jesus the promised powerful reign of God was about to break onto the scene of history.[3] Jesus reiterates this offer throughout the remainder of his ministry. Later, Jesus promises three of his disciples—Peter, James, and

---

1. Though the exact phrase "kingdom of God" is not found in the Old Testament, the concept is clearly present.
2. All biblical quotations are from the NIV 2011, unless otherwise noted.
3. Blomberg, *Jesus and the Gospels*, 270–71.

Introduction

John—that "some who are standing here will not taste death before they see that the kingdom of God has come with power" (Mark 9:1; see Matt 16:28; Luke 9:27). Furthermore, didn't Jesus, in his most extensive teaching on the future coming kingdom (Mark 13; Matt 24–25; Luke 21), instruct his disciples "Truly I tell you, this generation will certainly not pass away until all these things have happened" (Mark 13:30; see Matt 24:34; Luke 21:31)? And Jesus seemed to say that the Beloved Disciple (probably John) might still be alive when Jesus returns (John 21:22–23). Yet Jesus died, was raised, and then ascended into heaven, and the other disciples died without this promise of the kingdom coming in power and Jesus coming back apparently ever materializing.

Other New Testament authors also seem to speak as if the world could end with the coming of Christ in their lifetime. Paul reminds his Corinthian readers that "the time is short" (1 Cor 7:29). In Paul's most extended teaching on the coming of Christ he encourages the Thessalonian church with words that seem to suggest he and his readers might still be alive when Christ returns: "According to the Lord's word, we tell you that *we who are still alive*, who are left until the coming of the Lord . . . *we who are still alive and are left* will be caught up together with them in the clouds to meet the Lord in the air" (1 Thess 4:15–17). James encourages his readers to "be patient and stand firm, because the Lord's coming is near" (Jas 5:8), and Peter confidently proclaimed that "the end of all things is near" (1 Pet 4:7). The author of Hebrews called on his readers to encourage each other "as they see the day approaching" (Heb 10:25). In the very last book of the Bible, Revelation, which is the book most commonly associated with eschatology (teaching on the end-times), John promises that Jesus' coming and the events surrounding it will take place "soon" and are "near" (Rev 1:1, 3; 22:6, 10). John sees a vision of Babylon/Rome in chapter 17. Part of his vision is of a seven-headed beast. In 17:9–11, an angel tells John that the seven heads of the beast represent seven kings, probably Roman emperors. Yet John is told that five of those heads-kings have already passed, and he and his readers are living under the sixth king, with only one more (the seventh) to come before the end. Jesus himself promises once more at the end of the New Testament that he is coming *soon* (22:20). Surely, John and his readers had little time left. Passages like these from the Gospels and the rest of the New Testament could be multiplied, passages that seem to suggest that Jesus and other New Testament writers thought that the end of the world and the coming of Christ were about to take place—in their lifetime, or shortly thereafter. They were living on the brink of the end of the world.

Yet nearly two thousand years later, here we still are! Christ has still not returned and history still marches on. How do we account for passages in the New Testament such as those mentioned above, and some others, where the promises of the soon return of Christ do not seem to have materialized? How do we explain the expectation of the imminent arrival of the kingdom in Jesus' ministry and the expectation of the near return of Christ in the New Testament in the face of a long (at least from our perspective) delay? Where is the promise of his coming? (2 Pet 3:4). Was Jesus wrong in predicting the imminent inbreaking of the kingdom of God into history with his ministry? Were the New Testament authors mistaken in expecting the soon return of Christ, even in their lifetimes? Or were Jesus and the New Testament authors predicting something other than the arrival of the end-time kingdom?

As we have already noted, the church has always believed that history will draw to a close with the return of Christ to set up God's kingdom on earth ("He will come to judge the living and the dead"—The Apostle's Creed). But how do we explain the apparent failure of this event to transpire when New Testament authors seemed to think that it would happen right away? Is it "as though God's word has failed" (Rom 9:6)? Engaging these questions is of no little consequence. As Christopher M. Hays puts the problem bluntly, "If Jesus' prophecy about the timing of the kingdom's coming was not fulfilled, then isn't this Christianity thing really just all wrong?"[4] Hays' question gets right at the heart of the issue, and raises the question this book will attempt to answer. I have known Christians for whom this issue of the delay of Christ's coming has

---

4. Hays, *When the Son of Man Didn't Come*, 19.

Introduction

led them to conclude that the Bible was not completely trustworthy in all areas. How can we trust the Bible if its authors were mistaken on this critical point? Two thousand years is not "soon" in anyone's book. I have known others who have refused to believe in Christianity because of this issue: how can we trust someone who got it so wrong? "Isn't this Christianity thing really just all a joke?"

Consequently, there have been numerous attempts to provide some kind of an explanation for the issue of the delay of the parousia (coming) of Christ, when the New Testament seems to suggest that it should have happened soon, even in the lifetime of the first-century Christians. In the rest of this chapter, I only want to survey very briefly four possible explanations that have been popular responses to the apparent failure of the promised coming of Christ to establish his kingdom. The first three perspectives have been chosen because I often hear some form of one of these versions today, both in popular and more academic circles. The final perspective is chosen because it is represented in the first full book-length treatment of the issue of the delay of the coming of Christ to appear in some time. This will served as a starting point for examining what the New Testament texts have to say about the issue of the delay of the coming of Christ. The rest of this work will provide an alternative to these explanations.

PERSPECTIVES ON THE DELAY OF THE PAROUSIA

The "failed prophecy" view

According to some scholars and students of the Bible, Jesus and the New Testament authors simply missed the mark. They predicted the end of the world, the coming kingdom, and the return of Christ in their lifetime, and it simply did not happen as they thought it would. Though not always stated this bluntly, Jesus and the apostles flat out got it wrong! This was the perspective of an earlier theologian named Albert Schweitzer, who famously proposed that Jesus thought he would usher in the long-awaited kingdom of God, but he died rejected by God, disillusioned, and failing to bring that kingdom about.[5] More recently, a well-known New Testament scholar, Bart Ehrman, has reasserted this "failed prophecy" view, stating that Jesus predicted the imminent end of the world that did not happen.[6] Jesus was an apocalyptic prophet who got it wrong. The end never materialized as Jesus (and his followers) predicted. This view would certainly solve the problem of why Christ has not come back, but at a serious cost: the credibility of Jesus and his followers, and the reliability of the New Testament documents that Jesus' followers have authored. This perspective will obviously sit uncomfortably with those who hold to the Bible as the inspired word of God and believe in a God that supernaturally intervenes in history and can know the future. If the Bible is indeed the word of God, and if God does not lie, then the Bible and its writers could not have been wrong on this point. And if they were, does this not call the reliability of Scripture's teaching on this issue, and perhaps most other teachings, into serious question? Furthermore, if Jesus is the perfect revelation of God who spoke the truth from God, how could he have been so wrong on a matter of such importance?

The "fulfilled in A.D. 70" view

Another possible explanation that has become more popular recently, especially for much of Jesus' teaching in the Gospels, is that in many places where Jesus seemed to anticipate a coming end-of-the-world kingdom in his and his disciples' lifetime he was actually predicting the destruction of Jerusalem in A.D. 70. That is, when Jesus promised that his coming was near, or that some of his disciples would see the kingdom coming in power, he was referring to his coming to judge Jerusalem and its temple in history. This also may be what other New Testament authors anticipated when they thought the end was near (Jas 5:8; 1 Pet 5:7). Even in the

---

5. See Schweitzer, *Quest for the Historical Jesus*.
6. Ehrman, *Jesus: Apocalyptic Prophet*.

Introduction

book of Revelation, a book often credited with extensively dealing with the "end of the world," references to the soon return of Christ or scenes of judgment once again could refer to Christ coming to judge Jerusalem. At least that is how a few have understood it.[7] Therefore, Jesus and his disciples did indeed see the kingdom of God coming in power—in the form of God's judgment on Jerusalem and the temple in A.D. 70. Seen from this perspective, Jesus was not wrong, and his "coming" (in judgment upon Jerusalem) was indeed near and soon and it did happen in the lifetime of his disciples.

One of the more important and well-known advocates of this position is the New Testament scholar N. T. Wright. According to Wright, Jesus' statements about an imminent, apocalyptic coming were fulfilled in the coming of the Son of Man to judge Jerusalem.[8] The cosmic imagery of the darkening of the sun and moon, the falling stars and heaven being shaken (Mark 13:24–25) refers not to the end of history, but metaphorically to an earthly temporal event, the destruction of Jerusalem and its system of worship. Again, if Wright is correct, this would certainly solve the problem of how Jesus could predict a soon return and not be mistaken. Jesus did indeed come in judgment upon Jerusalem within the lifetime of his first followers. Jesus was not predicting his second coming at the end of history, but an event closer at hand.[9] There are certainly places where Jesus has this event in mind (see below on Matt 24; Mark 13; Luke 21). This would certainly provide a welcome alternative to the first view, that Jesus and his followers thought the world would end but were wrong. But whether this proposal fits all the references to Christ's future coming in the Gospels and the rest of the New Testament will need to be considered below. It still

---

7. The view that Revelation largely refers to events that transpire in the first century (especially the destruction of Jerusalem in A.D. 70) is known as the *preterist* View of Revelation.

8. Wright, *Jesus and the Victory of God*.

9. This does not mean that N. T. Wright and others who hold this view do not believe in a second coming of Christ at the end of history. It only means that they do not think this is what Jesus and other NT authors were predicting when they anticipate the soon or near coming of Christ.

seems that many of the passages that are sometimes taken to refer to this event in A.D. 70 are better seen as references to the second coming of Christ at the end of history.

The "classic dispensational" view

Dispensationalism is a theological system and method of interpreting Scripture. It tends to see God working in distinct ways with people in different periods of time, or dispensations. It also tends to draw a more or less sharp distinction between Israel and the church, as two peoples of God.[10] A couple of important issues for understanding its perspective of the coming of Christ are this movements' insistence that the Old Testament and New Testament be interpreted literally, and that the Old Testament promises of a political kingdom of David be fulfilled literally and physically to the people of Israel in the future. Israel will be restored to its land centered on a rebuilt temple, with the Messiah ruling over them (see Ezek 34–37). The classical dispensational view[11] sees Jesus in the Gospels offering the end-time coming of God's kingdom to earth in power, which was predicted in the Old Testament for the Jewish people. However, Jews in the first century rejected this offer of the kingdom, and because of the rejection by the Jewish nation, the prophetic clock was stopped and the promised theocratic kingdom was delayed and deferred into the indefinite future for a time when it will be offered once again to Israel at the second coming of Christ, and they will repent and receive it. At that time, Christ will set up the long-awaited messianic kingdom promised to the Jewish people in the Old Testament, on earth. This is usually understood by dispensationalists to take place during the time

---

10. Bateman IV, ed., *Three Central Issues in Contemporary Dispensationalism*.

11. Classical dispensationalism is to be distinguished from it more moderate sibling known as progressive dispensationalism. The latter still holds to a future for national Israel, but it sees the Old Testament promises of a coming messianic kingdom already being fulfilled spiritually in the church, more consistent with the "already"-but-"not-yet" tension of NT eschatology (see below). See Bock and Blaising, *Progressive Dispensationalism*.

Introduction

of the so-called millennial kingdom (the thousand-year reign) in Revelation 20:4–6. In between these two events—(a) Jesus' proclamation at his first coming of the coming earthy kingdom, which is delayed because of Jewish rejection, and (b) the fulfillment of that promised kingdom to Israel finally in the future at his second coming—we find the period of the church age. Rather than looking for the earthly kingdom and future coming of Christ to earth promised to Israel, the church is to wait for a "secret rapture" when Christ will return and take up the church to be with him (1 Thess 4:13–18). After the church is removed from earth in a rapture, the prophetic time-clock will start up again, and God will keep his promises to Israel of a coming, earthly kingdom, which was rejected and delayed at Christ's first coming, and offer this kingdom to Israel again. Therefore, the church awaits this "rapture," which will not be preceded by any signs, and which could happen at any time, "in the twinkling of an eye" (1 Cor 15:52).

According to the classic dispensational scheme, then, Jesus was not wrong in offering the kingdom during his lifetime—it was an actual offer; he merely withdrew the offer and delayed it for a later time because of Jewish unbelief and rejection. However, this still does not completely solve the problem for at least some New Testament texts, but only locates it elsewhere—in the so-called "rapture" of the church. In one sense the problem now becomes how New Testament authors, based on some of the texts we briefly noted above, could apparently think that *Jesus' coming to rapture the church* would come "soon" or was "near" (1 Pet 4:7), but it still has not yet taken place. Furthermore, the validity of this approach depends on accepting the entire dispensational scheme and its distinction between a rapture for the church and the second coming for the Jewish people. As the treatment of the texts below will demonstrate, we question whether this distinction is valid. We will take all of the references to the coming of Christ and to the end as a reference to the second coming of Christ; that is, the rapture and the second coming are the same event.

Where Is the Promise of His Coming?

The "conditional prophecy" view

The most complete and exhaustive treatment of this issue of the delay of the coming of Christ to date is a recent work by Christopher M. Hays in collaboration with several other scholars entitled, *When the Son of Man Didn't Come: A Constructive Proposal on the Delay of the Parousia*.[12] This work argues at great length that the offer of the kingdom by Jesus, as well as the expected soon return of Christ by other New Testament authors, is *conditioned* upon the response of repentance by humanity. That is, like many Old Testament prophecies of a coming kingdom (e.g., Jer 29:10–14; Dan 9:1–27), the promise of the return of Christ and his kingdom has been delayed due to the lack of repentance (notice the brief similarity with the dispensational view above); God is waiting for more people to repent (see 2 Pet 3:3–4, 8–12). In his sovereignty, God chooses to work in cooperation with the church and in response to his creation, to react to their decisions, actions, and repentance, to bring about his promised kingdom with the coming of his Messiah. Since the timing of Christ's coming depends on both divine *and human* action, the timing must therefore be open-ended. "*God can and has changed his mind about the timing of the eschaton in response to the work and shortcomings of the church.*"[13] Even where the New Testament does not explicitly link the promise of Christ's coming to repentance and the response of people, this condition is to be assumed to lie behind all the promises that Christ's coming is soon or near. Soon or near if people repent. This helpful and penetrating volume provides contributions from a number of important perspectives, biblical-exegetical, theological, philosophical, historical, in order to argue for the conditional nature of the New Testament author's expectations of a soon return of Christ, even in their lifetime. God has chosen to delay the coming of his Son, Jesus, because of the lack of sufficient response by his creation.

There is much that is helpful in this book. It leaves virtually no stone unturned in examining this issue. Once again, this would

---

12. Hays, *When the Son of Man Didn't Come*.
13. Hays, *When the Son of Man Didn't Come*, 264. Italics his.

Introduction

certainly be a welcome alternative to concluding that Jesus and the New Testament writers were wrong about their predictions of the near return of Christ. However, the authors of this volume have likely misread not a few texts, and while lack of repentance is certainly one of the key reasons for the delay of Christ's coming, it is not clear to me that it offers a complete solution. Nor is it clear to me that lack of repentance is always presented in the New Testament as the *cause* of the delay, and lack of repentance must be assumed to lie behind a number of texts.

SUMMARY

So where do we go from here? Where is the promise of his coming? The rest of this book will provide a detailed examination of the issue of the promises of the soon return of Christ and their apparent delay in the New Testament. The purpose of this book is not to provide a critique of the above proposed explanations of the delay of Christ's coming in the face of New Testament promises of Christ's quick return. Rather, this book will primarily focus on reading the key biblical texts that relate to the issue of the delay of the coming of Christ in light of the promises of his speedy return. It will provide a proposal that differs in various ways from all of the above explanations. Throughout this book we will use the term *parousia* to refer to the future second coming of Christ, Parousia being an English transliteration of a Greek term that means "presence" or "coming." It is the term that is usually used in the New Testament to refer to the future coming of Christ.

The first four chapters of this book will address the most important biblical texts that seem to predict the coming of Christ within the lifetime of his first hearers, texts that are frequently marshalled as proof that Jesus and other New Testament authors got it wrong. How do we account for such passages, when Jesus did not return within the lifetime of his followers (and two millennia later, he still has not come back)? One chapter will be devoted to passages from the Gospels that record statements of Jesus that seem to predict an immediate return. Two other chapters will be devoted to Acts and the letters of Paul, and to the General Epistles (Hebrews, James, 1–2 Peter, 1 John), and will examine passages in those New Testament sections that are relevant to the issue of the delay of the coming of Christ. Another single chapter will be devoted to the book of Revelation, a book that extensively deals with issues linked to the end and the coming of Christ. A final chapter will raise a couple of important theological issues related to the question of the delay of the coming of Christ, along with some pastoral reflections on this issue. The purpose of this book is to provide a balanced proposal for understanding these texts that promise the soon return of Christ in the face of delay and apparent non-fulfillment of these promises.

2

The Gospels

INTRODUCTION

The natural starting point logically and historically for our discussion is to consider the teaching of Jesus himself as recorded in the Gospels. As already noted, the central feature of Jesus' teaching was his proclamation that the long-awaited kingdom of God promised in the Old Testament Scriptures had finally arrived. All three Synoptic Gospels agree that this was the heart of Jesus' preaching from the outset of his adult ministry: "'The time has come,' he said. 'The kingdom of God has come near. Repent and believe the good news!'" (Mark 1:15; see Matt 3:17; Luke 4:43). But *in what sense* had the kingdom of God come near?

THE KINGDOM OF GOD IN JESUS' TEACHING

Before we look at any specific passages, it is important to understand what is meant by the phrase "kingdom of God." This will help us avoid a lot of potential misunderstanding when it comes to understanding Jesus' offer of a kingdom. When we think of the phrase "kingdom of God," we should not primarily think of a realm, or a political or geographical area (e.g., the United Kingdom) with borders and boundaries over which God rules. Nor should we see it primarily as corresponding to a period of time (e.g., the millennium). Rather, the term "kingdom" carries the more dynamic notion of "reigning" or "ruling," of God's sovereignty, his "kingly power."[1] Though the exact phrase "kingdom of God" does not occur in the Old Testament, the concept is certainly present. The Old Testament prophets anticipate a day when God's reign and rule will spread over the entire earth. God will one day rule over his people Israel, and over all the nations of the earth, through his Messiah (Ezek 34–37; Isa 60). His kingly rule will be a time of blessing and salvation for his people Israel, and all their enemies—the hostile nations (v. 12), evil, and death—will be defeated (Zech 14). All creation will be renewed (Isa 65:17–25). This brief survey provides the backdrop for what the first hearers would have expected when Jesus came proclaiming the good news of the nearness of the kingdom of God.

So in what sense is Christ foretelling the imminent arrival of this kingdom promised in the Old Testament, where Christ would rule over all people and renew all creation? In what sense was God's kingdom near? As we have already seen, some have concluded that Jesus was mistaken, and this kingdom as promised in the Old Testament never materialized as Jesus said it would. Instead, he was put to death for his beliefs. Classic dispensationalists concluded that Jesus offered precisely this earthly, theocratic kingdom, but that it was rejected by the Jewish nation, and so God "postponed" it for a later time (still apparently future at the time of this writing!). Others have argued that Jesus was referring to his coming in power to destroy Jerusalem in A.D. 70. A recent proposal has suggested that Jesus offered the end-time kingdom to his readers, but it has been delayed due to lack of repentance by the people. So how do we explain Jesus' preaching of the nearness of this kingdom, when it never arrived, at least in the way the Old Testament authors conceived of it? The rest of this chapter will examine a number of texts from the Gospels that appear to

---

1. Ladd, *Theology of the New Testament*, 63. There is widespread agreement by New Testament students and scholars that this is how "kingdom of God" should be understood.

The Gospels

refer to an expectation of the immediate, imminent arrival of the kingdom, as promised in the Old Testament, to be brought about by Jesus' coming.

MARK 1:15; MATTHEW 4:17; LUKE 4:43

Mark 1:15	Matthew 4:17	Luke 4:43
"The time has come," he said. "The kingdom of God has come near. Repent and believe the good news!"	From that time on Jesus began to preach, "Repent, for the kingdom of heaven has come near."	But he said, "I must proclaim the good news of the kingdom of God to the other towns also, because that is why I was sent."

According to these verses, at the very outset of his ministry Jesus clearly offered men and women the kingdom of God as promised in all those Old Testament texts. When Jesus said that the kingdom was "near" or "at hand," the Greek word is *engiken* (lit. "is in the state of being near"). This could imply either that the kingdom is near in the sense that it is imminent, but has not yet arrived (i.e., it is very close), or that it is near in the sense of already being present.[2] Probably we should understand this as saying that the kingdom is near in the sense that it is already dawning in the person of Jesus Christ; that it was within reach of men and women who would respond in faith to Jesus. It is doubtful that the solution to why it never came as described in the Old Testament is to say that Jesus was mistaken, or even with the classical dispensationalists that Jesus postponed the kingdom offer because of lack of Jewish response and belief, or that it was delayed or postponed because of failure of human response.

It was the late New Testament scholar George E. Ladd who popularized the view that the proper framework for understanding Jesus' offer of the kingdom of God in the Gospels was the tension between the "already" but "not yet."[3] That is, the offer by Jesus of the kingdom of God that was promised in the Old Testa-

---

2. France, *Gospel of Mark*, 91–93; Blomberg, *Matthew*, 73.
3. Ladd, *Theology of the New Testament*, 45–104.

ment was real, and was *"already" genuinely present* in the person and ministry of Jesus, but it would "not yet" come in its full, consummate form and manifestation until sometime in the future (at Christ's second coming). Some refer to this as realized eschatology. The end-time kingdom was already present in inaugurated and mystery form (see Matt 13), in advance of the future time when the kingdom would arrive in its full power. This accounts for elements in the Gospels where the kingdom of God seems to be near, or present (Mark 1:15; Matt 12:28), and other parts of the Gospels that seem to teach that the kingdom is still future (Matt 6:10: "Your kingdom come, your will be done on earth as it is in heaven"; Matt 25:31–46). It is not one or the other, present or future, but *both*.

Therefore, what Jesus offered at the outset of his ministry was not the final, full-blown form of the kingdom of God, but a partial and initial realization of it, in advance of a future, final form still to come. In fact, Jesus makes this abundantly clear elsewhere in the Gospels. His healing ministry and miracles were a demonstration that the kingdom of God had *already* arrived (Matt 4:23; 11:2–5). The fact that he cast out demons was proof that the powerful reign of God was *already* present. The classic text is Matthew 12:28: "But if it is by the Spirit of God that I drive out demons, then the kingdom of God has come upon you." By casting out demons the power of God's kingdom had already invaded the kingdom of Satan and evil and bound the strong man, in advance of a day in the future when God will defeat Satan for good and wipe out all evil (Rev 20:1–10).

Therefore, it is not necessary to conclude based on these passages above at the outset of Jesus' ministry that Jesus somehow got it wrong. Jesus did not offer the immediate arrival of the consummated, final form of the kingdom of God. Rather, Jesus came to offer the kingdom of God in partial, inaugurated form, while the final, ultimate fulfillment of the kingdom was still outstanding. The kingdom of God is "already" (at Jesus' first coming) while still "not yet" (until Jesus' second coming in the future). Men and women could already enter God's reign and rule and experience its blessing in the present, including deliverance from the power

The Gospels

of Satan, in advance of the consummation of that kingdom still to come in the future. Once more, this view is a staple of New Testament scholarship. But there are other sayings of Jesus that at first glance seem to be more problematic.

MARK 9:1; MATTHEW 16:28; LUKE 9:27

Mark 9:1	Matthew 16:28	Luke 9:27
And he said to them, "Truly I tell you, some who are standing here will not taste death before they see that the kingdom of God has come with power."	"Truly I tell you, some who are standing here will not taste death before they see the Son of Man coming in his kingdom."	"Truly I tell you, some who are standing here will not taste death before they see the kingdom of God."

In these three passages Jesus seems to suggest that at least some of his disciples would witness the arrival of the promised coming kingdom of God before they died: "some who are standing here will not taste death until they see the kingdom of God come with power" (Mark 9:1). Surely here if anywhere the reliability of Jesus' prediction could be called into question. After all, the powerful kingdom did not come, and Jesus and all his followers died without seeing the realization of Jesus' words. So did Jesus get it wrong?

At least some New Testament scholars think so. In his book *Jesus of Nazareth: Millenarian Prophet*, Dale Allison argues that Jesus' words here predict the imminent arrival of the kingdom in its fullness.[4] Yet Jesus' expectations of a coming, eschatological kingdom were not realized. For indeed Jesus and his followers did die without the parousia (Jesus' coming) arriving! In an earlier commentary on Matthew, Allison goes as far to admit that this view, that the coming kingdom in this saying refers to Jesus' second coming, entails the view that Matthew 16:28 contains a false prophecy.[5] Bart Ehrman has argued that readers must take

---

4. Allison, *Jesus of Nazareth*, 149–51.
5. Davies and Allison, *Matthew VIII–XVIII*, 679.

Where Is the Promise of His Coming?

Jesus' words in these verses at face value.[6] Jesus was an apocalyptic preacher who predicted imminent judgment and salvation, but this obviously did not materialize as Jesus predicted. In other words, Jesus was mistaken in his belief. According to Ehrman, one can even see other New Testament author's wrestling with this problem. Therefore, in Luke's version of this saying of Jesus (9:27) Luke removes the phrase "come in power." In other words, for Luke, Jesus no longer predicts the powerful, coming kingdom, but a present form of the kingdom. According to Ehrman, this was Luke's way of dealing with the delay of the coming kingdom.[7] If these scholars (and others) are right, then Jesus was mistaken, and this raises important questions about the reliability of Jesus' teaching more generally.

But is this how we should understand these words of Jesus? Was Jesus indeed falsely predicting the imminent end of the world and arrival of the eschatological kingdom? While it is *possible* that Jesus is here anticipating the end of the world in the lifetime of his disciples,[8] this is probably not how we should understand Jesus' words in these verses.

In all three of the Synoptic Gospels, Jesus says these words to his disciples in the context of a prediction of his coming suffering and death (Mark 8:31–38; Matt 16:21–26; Luke 9:21–26). In all three Gospels, Jesus' prediction of his death transitions into the implications of this for his disciples: they too must take up their cross and be willing to die for the sake of Christ. They may be called upon to literally "lose their life" for following Christ. But ironically, this is how they will gain life in the future (at the resurrection). Allegiance to Christ is more important than preservation of one's present, physical life. That brings us to the saying that is the focus of our attention: Jesus' coming in judgment provides the motivation for "taking up one's cross" and willingness to "loose one's life" in the present. Then come Jesus' problematic words: there are some standing in Jesus' midst who will not die (martyrdom?)

6. Ehrman, *Jesus: Apocalyptic Prophet*, 18.
7. Ehrman, *Jesus: Apocalyptic Prophet*, 130.
8. Gundry, *Matthew*, 341–42.

The Gospels

before they see the kingdom/Son of Man coming in glory and power. Furthermore, all three Gospels agree by placing these words immediately before an important event: the transfiguration of Jesus (Mark 9:2-13; Matt 17:1-13; Luke 9:28-36).

There are a number of ways that one could understand this saying of Jesus in Mark 9:1 (and Matt 16:28; Luke 9:27), which are preferable to taking it as a prediction that the end of the world would come in some of his disciples' lifetime, a prediction that was erroneous.[9]

1. It is possible that Jesus' words refer to Jesus' resurrection and exaltation. In Acts 2, for example, Jesus' resurrection and exaltation to heaven are seen as his enthronement as Messiah-king in fulfillment of the Old Testament promises (Acts 2:31-36; see Eph 1:19-22). So some standing in Jesus' presence would still be alive when he was raised and exalted to heaven. But this view is a little more difficult to sustain in view of the "*some* who are standing here," for *all* the disciples (except for Judas) did in fact witness to Christ's resurrection and his exaltation.

2. It is possible that Jesus' words refer to the Day of Pentecost when the Holy Spirit came powerfully upon the followers of Christ (Acts 2). Certainly the quotation from Joel 2 in Acts 2:17-21 makes this view attractive, as Joel 2 anticipates the pouring out of the Spirit in the future day of the Lord. Again, however, *all* Jesus' disciples would indeed survive to witness this event. Like the first option, this view has a slight difficulty with the "some" of Jesus' statement.

3. Another possibility is that the coming of the kingdom/Son of Man refers to the destruction of Jerusalem in A.D. 70. As seen above, this is a popular explanation for many of Jesus' predictions of the nearness of his coming. This could certainly make sense, especially since later on Jesus will address the issue of the destruction of Jerusalem (Mark 13; Matt 24-25; Luke 21). But would this event by itself best be described as the kingdom of God coming in

---

9. For a survey of possible proposals for understanding this saying based on Mark 9:1 see Brower, "Mark 9:1: Seeing the Kingdom," 17-41.

Where Is the Promise of His Coming?

power? Furthermore, the context does not offer any clear indications that Jesus is referring to the destruction of Jerusalem.

4. A likely option is that this saying refers to the transfiguration of Jesus. What this view has going for it is that in all three Gospels the account of the transfiguration follows hard on the heels of this saying of Jesus. This view makes good sense of the context, especially given the placement of the transfiguration right after the saying that some would not die until they saw the Son of May/kingdom of God coming in power.[10] Some object to this identification, because it does not make sense of the temporal phrase that begins the transfiguration account: "After six days" (Mark 9:2; Matt 17:1); "About eight days" (Luke 9:28). It seems like a ridiculous stretch for Jesus to say that some standing there would not taste death, if the event being referred to takes place only one week later! *Of course* they would still be alive![11] However, in fact only *some* (only three of the twelve) of the disciples did witness the event of the transfiguration of Jesus, "and the rest of them would indeed 'taste death' without seeing anything comparable."[12]

There are other connections between this saying of Jesus that he would come in power, and the transfiguration. The description of Jesus' transformation and radiant appearance certainly seems to fit the language of the kingdom of God/Son of Man coming in power (see Dan 7:9; 10:5–6; Rev 1:13–16). There are other hints that this event is to be associated with the coming, eschatological kingdom. The presence of Moses and Elijah carries eschatological significance. Deuteronomy 18:15–19 promises a coming prophet like Moses, and in Malachi 4:5 Elijah would return in the last days.[13] "The reappearance of these two great figures of the past

---

10. Blomberg, *Matthew*, 261.

11. Hagner, *Matthew 14–28*, 486; Brower, "Mark 9:1: Seeing the Kingdom," 23.

12. France, *Gospel of Mark*, 345. The disciples did see Jesus resurrected, but still not in the dazzling display of glory and power in which he appeared in his transfiguration.

13. France, *Gospel of Matthew*, 648.

The Gospels

thus symbolizes the coming of the long-expected messianic age."[14] Peter's desire to set up three booths is probably a reference to the celebration of the Feast of Tabernacles. The Feast of Tabernacles, one of the key feasts celebrated by Israel (along with Passover and Unleavened Bread), celebrated God's deliverance of his people in the wilderness (Exod 23:16; 34:22; Lev 23:42-43), but it also anticipated a future, eschatological deliverance (Zech 14:16-21). The fact that this transfiguration takes place on a "high mountain" may also be significant, in that visions of the return of God in glory to bring salvation to his people occur on a mountain (Ezek 40:2; Rev 21:10). The presence of a "cloud" at the transfiguration also has eschatological overtones, in that it is associated with the coming of a Son of Man figure (Dan 7:13; Rev 1:7). Added up, what this all means is that the transfiguration itself is a foretaste, a proleptic experience, of the coming of the kingdom of God/Son of Man in power in the future. The transfiguration is "a foreshadowing of the future glorious coming.... The transfiguration will be a glorious experience (17:2, 5), but it will only be a temporary preview of what will come with permanence when Jesus returns to the earth."[15] In this way, some of the disciples did indeed see the kingdom of God and the Son of Man coming with power, not in its final glorious form, but in a way that anticipated that final glorious arrival.

5. Some would say that Jesus had two or more of the above events in mind, when he predicted the coming kingdom of God in power. For example, one commentator, Darrell L. Bock, opts for a combination of 1 and 4 above.[16] D. A. Carson thinks that the reference is far more general, and just refers to "the manifestation of Christ's kingly reign exhibited after the resurrection in a host of ways, not the least of them being the rapid multiplication of disciples and the mission to the Gentiles."[17] Whether Carson's view

---

14. France, *Gospel of Mark*, 352.

15. Turner, *Matthew*, 413. See also France, *Gospel of Mark*, 345.

16. Bock, *Luke 1:1—9:50*, 859. Keener, *Gospel of Matthew*, 436 n. 106: "Probably the transfiguration proleptically introduces the whole eschatological sphere, which Jesus' resurrection inaugurates and his return consummates."

17. Carson, "Matthew," 434.

also rules out a reference to the transfiguration, Christ's resurrection-exaltation, Pentecost, or the destruction of the Jerusalem is not clear, and his view overlooks the close connection between this saying and the transfiguration within the text of all three Gospels. But the point would still stand: Jesus' prediction that some standing in his midst would not die before they saw the coming of the kingdom and Son of Man in power should not be taken as a reference to the parousia, the coming of Christ at the end of the age (i.e., his second coming). Jesus did not erroneously predict the arrival of the earthly kingdom in all its power and glory. Rather, no matter which of the above options (or combinations) one settles on (and I have given the nod to the view that Jesus is referring to his transfiguration), Jesus is referring to an event that did indeed take place within the lifetime of his disciples. This also fits perfectly with the observation already made, that with Jesus' own person and ministry, the kingdom of God was already being inaugurated in advance of its future fulfillment.

MATTHEW 10:23

> When you are persecuted in one place, flee to another. Truly I tell you, you will not finish going through the towns of Israel before the Son of Man comes. (Matt 10:23)

This saying, which is unique to Matthew, is probably one of the most difficult to explain,[18] in terms of Jesus' prediction of the coming Son of Man at the end of history to set up his kingdom, which then never apparently transpired. In this verse, Jesus predicts that his disciples will not have made their way through all the towns of Israel in their mission before the Son of Man returns. This saying occurs within a larger section where Jesus commissions and then instructs his disciples regarding the mission on which he sends them (10:1—11:1). In this regard, it would appear that Jesus prom-

---

18. Carson says it "is among the most difficult in the NT canon" ("Matthew," 290).

The Gospels

ises to return before the twelve disciples, whom he commissions and instructs, complete their mission. If this is the case, Jesus' parousia or second coming never materializes, and Jesus was once more mistaken. However, before jumping to this conclusion too quickly, there are a few things that need to be factored in. There seems to be a difference in perspective in the discourse starting with 10:17. While verses 1–16 fit comfortably within the immediate mission of the twelve disciples in Galilee during Jesus' ministry, starting with verse 17 and following the perspective becomes much broader than the specific mission of the twelve disciples.[19] In verses 5–15, the disciples are restricted to a mission to Israel, but starting with verse 17 their mission now expands to include gentiles, where they will stand before "governors" and "kings" (see verse 18). Furthermore, the persecution they will face in these verses goes beyond anything they experienced during Jesus' time with them[20] (see the book of Acts). In other words, verses 17–42 most likely predict events that will transpire after Jesus' death and resurrection and assume a more widespread mission. Another way of putting it is that Jesus addresses a short-term mission in 10:1–16, and then a longer-term mission in 10:17–42. It is in this context of a longer-term mission after Jesus' resurrection that verse 23 must be understood. So what is Jesus predicting here?

The famous German theologian, Albert Schweitzer, popularized the view that in 10:23 Jesus thought the end would come soon, and that the disciples would not finish their mission to Israel before the Son of Man returned to set up his kingdom.[21] But Jesus was wrong in his prediction, thought Schweitzer; he died, and the end never came. Following this, it has been common for interpreters to conclude that Jesus predicted the end of the world in his disciples' lifetime but was mistaken about its timing. However, as seen above, this prediction of Jesus in verse 23 occurs within the

---

19. France, *Gospel of Matthew*, 389. See also Carson, "Matthew," 282. Blomberg, *Matthew*, 174: "With v. 17 Jesus shifts to predictions that were not fulfilled in the immediate mission of the Twelve."

20. Carson, "Matthew," 282.

21. Schweitzer, *Quest for the Historical Jesus*.

23

Where Is the Promise of His Coming?

more long-term commission of Jesus' disciples, perhaps including the twelve but even beyond just the twelve. There are a number of possibilities for interpreting this saying. I will only consider three solutions to how we should understand the coming of the Son of Man that will bring to an end the disciples' mission to Israel.

First, Richard T. France entertains the possibility that the coming of the Son of Man in 10:23 refers to the resurrection of Jesus, after which the mission to Israel ends, and the followers of Jesus are now commanded by the *resurrected* Christ to make disciples of all nations (not just Israel) in Matthew 28:18–20.[22] However, speaking of the coming of the Son of Man would seem an odd way of referring to the resurrection. Furthermore, this ignores the context of persecution in verses 17–42 which seems to take one beyond anything the disciples experienced before Christ's resurrection.

Second, another option is that 10:23 refers to the coming of the Son of Man in judgment against Jerusalem (A.D. 70). This is possible, since we have seen that for Jesus (and Matthew) eschatology is realized, that is, it comes in inaugurated, partial form in advance of its final manifestation. Thus, the coming of Jesus in judgment on Jerusalem could be an example of the "already" aspect of the coming of the Son of Man. Furthermore, this would fit the context of verses 17–42, which refer to events that occur after the ministry of Jesus, including the destruction of Jerusalem in A.D. 70. Finally, it would also fit the reference to "the cities of Israel." The disciples, in their mission, will not finish evangelizing Israel before God comes in judgment on Israel.[23] In this way, Jesus expresses the urgency of the mission of his disciples to Israel. It is entirely possible that Jesus (and Matthew) is referring to the destruction of Jerusalem in A.D. 70. However, the promise of salvation to the one who stands firm to the "end" (v. 22) and the broader context of persecution at the hands of the gentiles (vv. 18–19) might envision a wider situation that will characterize the entire period of the church age

---

22. France, *Gospel of Matthew*, 398.
23. Carson, "Matthew," 293.

until Christ's second coming. In either case, Jesus would not be mistaken regarding his coming.

Third, Jesus' words in verse 23 could indeed refer to the second coming of the Son of Man at the end of history. The saying that "those who remain faithful to the end will be saved" in the immediately preceding verse (v. 22) favors a reference to the second coming of Christ in verse 23 as well. But this does not mean that Jesus was then mistaken. Jesus' saying should once more be understood within the context of the longer-term mission in verses 17–42. During their broader, more long-term mission, the disciples will not finish their mission to Israel before the Son of Man returns. In this case, Jesus predicts his return before this broader mission of his followers comes to an end with reference to their mission to Israel. Thus, alongside of their work with the gentiles, Jesus envisions an ongoing work with Israel, even in the face of persecution.[24] Jesus, then, is not predicting when the return will take place, but envisions the coming of the Son of Man before their mission is complete. In fact, Matthew ends in 28:18–20 with the resurrected Jesus commanding his disciples to make disciples of *all nations* (including Israel), so that Jesus (and Matthew) still views the mission of the disciples (and Matthew's readers) as outstanding and incomplete.

The promise of a broader mission to the gentiles in 10:23 (and 28:18–20) suggests some period of time will elapse, but that it could be cut off at any time by the Son of Man's coming (the "end of the age" in 28:20). Obviously neither Jesus nor his disciples anticipated a two-thousand-year gap, but neither does Jesus' saying in 10:23 *require* that he come back within the lifetime of his disciples, so that his failure to do so renders his words mistaken. Once the broader mission is underway, the Son of Man could return at any time. It is possible that we should understand Jesus' words "as a reference to the perpetually incomplete Jewish mission.... But they must keep at it throughout the entire church age."[25] Jesus is

---

24. Gundry, *Matthew*, 194, though Gundry thinks the saying was composed by Matthew to ensure that the mission to Israel continued.

25. Blomberg, *Matthew*, 176.

Where Is the Promise of His Coming?

ensuring that along with their mission to the gentiles his followers do not give up on evangelizing Jews despite persecution. They must persevere in their mission until the Son of Man returns.[26] In this sense, the statement is not so much a prediction as an imperative to not give up proclaiming the gospel of the kingdom to Israel. While there is much to be said for the third interpretation above, either of the last two understandings of this verse make it unlikely that Jesus is mistakenly predicting his second coming at the end of history in the lifetime of his disciples.

MARK 13:30; MATTHEW 24:34; LUKE 21:32, AND MARK 13:24; MATTHEW 24:29; LUKE 21:25

Mark 13:30	Matthew 24:34	Luke 21:32
Truly I tell you, this generation will certainly not pass away until all these things have happened.	Truly I tell you, this generation will certainly not pass away until all these things have happened.	Truly I tell you, this generation will certainly not pass away until all these things have happened.

Mark 13:24	Matthew 24:29	Luke 21:25
But in those days, following that distress, "the sun will be darkened, and the moon will not give its light . . ."	Immediately after the distress of those days "the sun will be darkened, and the moon will not give its light; the stars will fall from the sky, and the heavenly bodies will be shaken."	There will be signs in the sun, moon and stars. On the earth, nations will be in anguish and perplexity at the roaring and tossing of the sea.

Another important text that seems to suggest that Jesus thought that the end of the world would come in his and his disciples' lifetime is the saying that comes in the so-called eschatological (or Olivet) discourse of Jesus found in Mark 13, Matthew 24–25, and

---

26. See Keener, *Gospel of Matthew*, 325.

The Gospels

Luke 21. We will not consider all the details of the entire discourse, but will focus on the sayings of Jesus that are in question. But in treating those specific verses we will refer to larger segments of the discourse where necessary. However, a brief summary is in order. The disciples' observation about the impressive structure of the temple provides the occasion for Jesus' to predict the destruction of the temple. The disciples then ask in response when this event will transpire. Jesus answers their question by focusing on two key events: the destruction of Jerusalem and its temple, and the coming of the Son of Man. Jesus also warns his readers not to be deceived by numerous events that could be taken as signs that his coming was near: wars, rumors of wars, earthquakes, and famines. The crucial question is the relationship and timing of these events. We will try to unravel some of this in the following section.

The words of Jesus in question come after Jesus describes signs that will precede his coming, including the destruction of Jerusalem, the cosmic events that will actually accompany his coming (the Greek word here is *parousia*), and the parable of the fig tree. Jesus says, "Truly I tell you, this generation will certainly not pass away until all these things have happened" (Mark 13:30). It appears that once more Jesus thought that his coming in power to bring the consummated kingdom of God would happen immediately, within the lifetime of his disciples ("this generation"). They would see all these things happen. But obviously this did not transpire. His disciples passed from the scene without ever witnessing the events of the second coming described in Mark 13:23–27, Matthew 24:29–31, and Luke 21:25–28. And two thousand years later we are apparently still waiting for this grand event. So what do we make of these words of Jesus? Certainly, if anywhere in the Gospels Jesus could be seen to be mistaken and his reliability called into question it would be here.

A common approach to this verse that does not entail seeing it as a failed prediction of Christ's second coming is to see the events in this entire section of the discourse as referring to the destruction of Jerusalem in A.D. 70.[27] In addition to the clear

---

27. France, *Gospel of Matthew*, 929–30; Wright, *Jesus and the Victory of*

reference to this event in Mark 13:14–20 (Matt 24:15–22; Luke 21:20–24), the description of Christ coming on the clouds and the breakup of the constellations in Mark 13:23–27 (Matt 24:29–31; Luke 21:25–28) could refer symbolically to the coming of the Son of Man in judgment upon Jerusalem in A.D. 70. Those that hold this position point to Old Testament texts where similar language to that used here by Jesus is used of God's *temporal, historical judgment* of nations (e.g., Joel 1–2).[28] In the same way, it is argued, Jesus uses such imagery to refer to his coming and the breakup of the constellations to depict his judgment on Jerusalem (in A.D. 70). The word "coming" is often associated with "second coming" by most Christians, but it literally only means "presence" or "arrival."[29] According to this view, Jesus' arrival or presence in the eschatological discourse is for the purpose of judgment of Jerusalem. Jesus' followers (this generation) did indeed witness this "coming" in their lifetime. Andrew Perriman sees the "coming" of Jesus Christ as consisting of two levels: the vindication of Jesus as the suffering Son of Man (Daniel 7) in the destruction of Jerusalem, but also the vindication of the saints, the church, as the new people of God in the world.[30]

While there is much to be said for interpreting this saying of Jesus in the context of the world-changing events of A.D. 70, a more likely view sees Jesus as predicting that his disciples would indeed witness all these things happening, including the destruction of Jerusalem, but understands "all these things" in a more general way. The event described in Mark 13:23–27 (and Matt 24:29–32; Luke 21:25–28) does indeed refer to the second coming of Christ, but the "all these things" in the saying of Jesus in question does not refer to the second coming of Christ but to something else. In their context, the "all these things" in Mark 13:30 (Matt 24:34; Luke 21:32) refers back to the saying right before it: "Even so, when you see *these things* happening, you know that it is near,

---

God, 339–68.

28. Wright, *Jesus and the Victory of God*, 339–68.

29. Wright, *Jesus and the Victory of God*, 341.

30. Perriman, *Coming of the Son of Man*, 63–64.

The Gospels

right at the door" (Mark 13:29; see Matt 24:33; Luke 21:28). More specifically, the "all these things" in Mark 13:30 (Matt 24:34; Luke 21:32) refers to the "these things" in Mark 13:4, 29 (Matt 24:33; Luke 21:28).[31] But what are the "all/these things" referring to? It is tempting to take it as a reference to the immediately preceding verses (Mark 13:23–27; Matt 24:29–32; Luke 21:25–28), which refer to the second coming of Christ: the darkening of the sun and moon, the breakup of the constellations, and the appearance of the Son of Man in the sky and coming in power on the clouds. However, this would create a difficulty; Jesus' statement would be an odd tautology: "when you see the coming of the Son of Man, know that the coming of the Son of Man is right at the door!" In other words, when the Son of Man actually returns, it would not make much sense to say that his coming is still right at the door!

Therefore, it is more likely that the "all/these things" refer back to all the signs that Jesus describes in the prior verses: wars, rumors of wars, earthquakes, famines, and the rise of false "Messiahs" (Mark 13:7–23; Matt 24:6–26; Luke 21:9–21).[32] This also includes one particularly disastrous event: the destruction of Jerusalem in A.D. 70 (Mark 13:14–20; Matt 24:15–22; Luke 21:20–24). All of these would be the referent of "all/these things." In fact, the disciples did witness all of this in their lifetime. What, then, is Jesus saying? When all of these things happen, Christ will return. But Jesus' words do not demand that he comes back within the lifetime of his disciples. In only means that *once all these events take place, Jesus can come back at any time.* As Adrio König summarizes, "they are signs of Christ's imminent return which have accompanied the church in its course through history and have summoned it to unceasing vigilance."[33] That is, these are signs that throughout the entire age call the church to preparedness and watchfulness, as the parables of Jesus in the rest of Matthew 24–25 call for, not signs that predict *when* exactly Christ will return.

---

31. Witherington III, *Jesus, Paul and the End of the World*, 42.

32. Blomberg, *Matthew*, 364; Carson, "Matthew," 569; Osborne, *Matthew*, 899.

33. Konig, *Eclipse of Christ in Eschatology*, 190.

Where Is the Promise of His Coming?

Jesus goes on and provides further perspective on the timing of his return. Perhaps the most programmatic statement is found in Mark 13:32 (see Matt 24:36): "But about that day or hour no one knows, not even the angels in heaven, nor the Son, but only the Father." When *all these things* take place, the Son of Man can return at *any* time. But since no one knows the day or hour, things could go on for some time.

This is reinforced in Matthew's Gospel in a series of parables that Jesus teaches. There are two important parables told by Jesus in chapters 24 and 25 that provide a balanced perspective on the coming of Christ. The first parable in 24:45–51 is of a master and a faithful vs. a wicked steward. The master goes on a trip and leaves things in the hands of two stewards. The first steward is found faithful when the master returns. But the second (wicked) steward sees things differently. The key is that he thinks "My master is staying away a long time" (v. 48). And the steward begins to act irresponsibly. What happens next is that the master comes back *sooner than the steward thought* (v. 50: "on a *day* he does not expect him and at an *hour* he is not aware of"; notice the repetition of "day" and "hour" from 24:36)! The steward was not prepared for the *imminent* arrival of his master, as he was used to the delay.

But this perspective is balanced by the next parable in Matthew 25:1–13: The Parable of the Ten Maidens. In this parable, ten maidens are divided into two groups, five which are described as foolish, and five which are described as wise. Both are waiting for the arrival of the bridegroom in the context of a first-century wedding. What distinguishes the foolish from the wise maidens? The issue they face is found in verse 5: "the bridegroom was a *long time* in coming." That is, the bridegroom *delayed*, the point being that the five foolish maidens were not prepared for the delay (they did not have enough oil to keep their lamps burning for very long), while the five wise were prepared for delay with extra oil. This provides a balance to the previous parable. The two parables address opposite problems; in the first parable the master comes back sooner than the servant thinks, while in the second parable the bridegroom delays longer than the maidens think. And the issue is

The Gospels

being prepared for either scenario. Applied to the return of Christ after "all/these things have happened," Christ might come back sooner than we think (Matt 24:45–51), or he might delay longer than we think (Matt 25:1–13). No one knows. Jesus calls for his followers to be prepared for either scenario. In other words, Jesus at least makes provision for a possible delay, making it unlikely that Jesus' earlier words in 24:34 refer to a prediction of Jesus' coming within the lifetime of the disciples. To put it all together: when Jesus' disciples see all these things take place (wars, rumors of wars, famines, earthquakes, false Messiahs, and the events leading to and including the destruction of Jerusalem in A.D. 70), they should know that the Son of Man's coming is right at the door. But since no one knows the day or hour, the return of Christ *may take place immediately, or there may be a delay*. Jesus' followers must be *ready for either scenario*, as his parables warn. Therefore, although Jesus does not anticipate anything like a two-thousand-year delay, nothing in this saying of Jesus requires that he is mistakenly predicting his return within the lifetime of his disciples.

Within the same discourse Jesus makes another statement that could be construed as a prediction of his coming within the lifetime of the disciples, which then failed to materialize. The starkest form of the statement is found in Matthew 24:29: "Immediately after the distress of those days, the sun will be darkened and the moon will not give its light, the stars will fall from the heavens, and the powers of the heavens will be shaken" (see also Mark 13:24; Luke 21:25).[34] The key issue is, what is the "distress of those days," after which the event in verse 29 (the breakup of the constellations) will immediately take place? Before answering that question, we must figure out what event is being referred to with the sun and moon being darkened, and stars falling, and the powers of heaven being shaken in verse 29. While it is common for some

---

34. Mark 13:24 has the more general "in those days, after that distress," which gives no indication of the immediacy of the coming of Christ in relationship to the destruction of Jerusalem in A.D. 70. Luke 21:25 is even more vague, and says "and there will be signs in the sun and moon and stars . . . ." So the issue of "failed prophecy" is not as sharp of an issue as it is in Matthew 24:29. Therefore, we will focus primarily on Matthew's version of the saying.

31

to take this as a metaphorical reference to the coming of Christ in judgment upon Jerusalem in A.D. 70, I suggested above that it is probably a reference to the second coming of Christ at the end of history. This seems to me to be the best way to account for such language. So what is the "distress of those days" that the coming of Christ will immediately follow? In the context, the clearest option would seem to be to take it as referring to the event just described in verses 15–22. This is a clear reference to the events leading up to and including the destruction of Jerusalem in A.D. 70. Notice that this event is referred to as "great distress (tribulation)" (v. 21) and as "those days" (v. 22). If this is the case, Jesus appears to be predicting his return immediately after the events of A.D. 70, which obviously did not happen.

However, we should probably put the pieces of this puzzle together another way. Some have suggested that at this point Jesus broadens out to focus on the "end time" tribulation period just prior to his second coming.[35] However, there is no indication in the context that Jesus skips to the very end of history to refer to a final period of great tribulation just prior to the return of Christ. We saw above that it is possible that the reference to the sun and moon not shining, and the stars falling, refers to the coming of Jesus in judgment upon Jerusalem in A.D. 70. The events in verses 15–28 refer to the seize of Jerusalem, and then verse 29 refers to the final blow: the coming of Jesus in judgment upon Jerusalem's *temple*.[36] Despite the increasing popularity of this view, it will be assumed here, as already explained, that the cosmic language in verse 29 is a reference to the second coming of Christ.[37] Jesus' words in Matthew 24:29 seem to refer to a distinct event after the distress of "those days" (vv. 15–28), since "those days" will be "cut short" (v. 22). So how does Jesus' return come "immediately after the distress of those days"? It is likely that the "distress of those

---

35. See Osborne, *Matthew*, 893.

36. France, *Matthew*, 919–20.

37. See Blomberg, *Matthew*, 362–63; Carson, "Matthew," 548–58; Keener, *Gospel of Matthew*, 584–85; Osborne, *Matthew*, 893 for arguments for this perspective.

The Gospels

days" refers not only to the destruction of Jerusalem, but to the entire period of distress (tribulation) referred to in verses 4–28, which includes the destruction of Jerusalem in verses 15–22.[38] The word "distress (tribulation)" in verse 29 is also found in verse 9. The time of distress is also referred to as "the beginning of birthpangs" (v. 8), which suggests that there are still more to come. The destruction of Jerusalem in verses 15–22 is but one intense example of the tribulation that will characterize the entire period depicted in verses 4–28. It is immediately after those days (including, but not exclusively, the destruction of Jerusalem in A.D. 70) that the coming of the Son of Man will take place. But once more, Jesus is silent as to how long the period of "birth pangs" will last, only that Jesus will return following this period of distress in verses 4–28.

So it is unlikely that Matthew 24:29 is a prediction that Jesus would return in the lifetime his disciples, a prediction that was consequently erroneous. Instead, Jesus is indeterminate as to the precise timing of his coming. All that we know from Matthew 24 is that Jesus will return after a period of distress. But as Jesus reminds us, "No one knows the day or the hour." Of course, Jesus and his disciples did not envision an interval of two millennia. But neither would the disciples have insisted that Jesus *must* come back in their lifetime. Jesus' followers simply did not know, and must be prepared for both imminency (24:45–51) and possible delay (25:1–13), since "[e]verything necessary to prepare for this Parousia (Christ's return) will occur within the lifetime of Jesus' disciples."[39] It is important to recognize that Jesus' intention within the entire discourse of Matthew 24–25 (and Mark 13; Luke 21) is hortatory. Especially as the parables in Matthew 24–25 show, Jesus' main concern is to foster vigilance and responsible living in light of Christ's return, not to predict how close to the end he and his disciples are.

---

38. Blomberg, *Matthew*, 361–62; Carson, "Matthew," 557, 567.
39. Blomberg, *Matthew*, 352.

Where Is the Promise of His Coming?
JOHN 21:22

> Jesus answered [Peter], "If I want him [the beloved disciple] to remain alive until I return, what is that to you? You must follow me." (John 21:22)

This saying of Jesus, which occurs at the very end of John's Gospel, also seems to suggest at first glance that Jesus thought he would return in his (and his disciples') lifetime. When Peter sees the disciple identified as the "disciple Jesus loved,"[40] Peter draws attention to him (vv. 20–21), perhaps wondering if he will undergo death in the same way he (Peter) will—martyrdom (v. 19). Jesus then replies to Peter with these words, "'If I want him to remain until I come,' Jesus answered, 'what is that to you? As for you, follow me'" (v. 22). In other words, "in brief, Peter is told it is none of his business."[41] But what is Jesus saying about the destiny of the beloved disciple? It appears that Jesus is suggesting that the beloved disciple may very well be alive ("remain") at the second coming of Christ. And it looks like this may be how some in the author's day took this saying according to verse 23: "So the word went out to the believers [lit. brothers] that this disciple would not die." It is doubtful that some thought that the disciple would never die, and live for hundreds of years. Rather, they thought he would not die before Christ returned. In other words, some apparently thought that, based on this saying of Jesus, Christ would return within the lifetime of the beloved disciple. Perhaps with each passing year and the advancing age of the beloved disciple, the eschatological enthusiasm heightened.[42] Or if the beloved disciple were already dead, perhaps some wondered at the truthfulness of Jesus' words.

In any case, the rest of verse 23 is the correction by the author of chapter 21 to such misunderstandings of these words of Jesus: "but Jesus did not say that he [the beloved disciple] would not die,

---

40. For now I will forego discussion on the precise identity of the "disciple whom Jesus loved" (the beloved disciple). But a good case can be made, I think, for the Apostle John as responsible for the work.
41. Carson, *Gospel according to John*, 681.
42. Carson, *Gospel according to John*, 682.

but, 'If I want him to stay until I come, what is that to you'?" That is, Jesus' words should not be taken as a guarantee that he will return within the lifetime of the beloved disciple. It appears that the author's response in verse 23 highlights the conditional nature of Jesus' words ("if I want him to stay"): Jesus' may want the beloved disciple to be alive still (in contrast to Jesus' plans for Peter) when he returns. But this leaves open the possibility that the disciple might die before Jesus returns. In response to Peter, then, Jesus entertains the *possibility* that the beloved disciple would remain alive until the coming of Christ, but not the certainty that he necessarily will. Jesus' whole point was that whether through martyrdom (Peter), or remaining alive for some time (the beloved disciple), perhaps even until the second coming, both are called by Jesus to "follow me" (vv. 19, 22). Perhaps this saying should not be taken so much as a precise eschatological statement, but more as a rebuke to Peter: "It is none of your business, Peter, what happens to the beloved disciple. Why, if I want, I could allow him to still be alive when I return (if I choose to return in his lifetime). That is none of your concern. Just follow me!" So once more, these words at the conclusion of John's Gospel cannot be taken as a failed prediction of the return of Christ in the first century. Like other sayings of Jesus, it allows for the possibility of Christ's coming taking place within the lifetime of his disciples. But it does not exclude the fact that there could be some delay. Peter and the beloved disciple simply did not know, and instead needed to focus attention on the more important issue: "follow me."

CONCLUSION

The coming kingdom of God was an important part of Jesus' preaching during his earthly ministry. The kingdom of God that Jesus offered has as its backdrop the promised reign of God and his appointed king (the Messiah) in the Old Testament. However, when Jesus initially preaches the arrival of the kingdom, he offered an inaugurated form of the kingdom which stopped short of its full consummation yet to come in the future. In other words, men and women could already experience the reign of God and its attendant blessings (e.g., release from the power of Satan), in advance of a day when it would arrive in all its fullness. In the Gospels we find Jesus teaching on both: the already and the not-yet aspect of the kingdom of God.

There are a number of sayings that could be construed as Jesus predicting his soon return within the lifetime of his first-century disciples, with the conclusion that Jesus was wrong, since he never returned. However, the above study has tried to demonstrate that none of these statements should be taken as Jesus predicting that he would return immediately, a prediction that was in error. Instead, these sayings indicate only the *possibility* that Jesus would return within the lifetime of his followers. At least one saying probably does refer to an event that will occur within the lifetime of Jesus followers, where only some (three) saw him transfigured (Mark 9:1; Matt 16:28; Luke 9:27). Yet Jesus' teaching also includes the possibility of delay. While Jesus, and the Gospel writers, do not envision a two-thousand-year gap, the two parables found in Matthew 24:45–51 and 25:1–13 balance imminence and delay: Christ might come back sooner than they think, or he might delay longer than they think. Jesus' commission to the disciples at the end of Matthew's Gospel, to make disciples of all nations (Matt 28:18–20; see 24:14), assumes some measure of delay for the commission to be carried out. Jesus' own words may summarize the broader perspective that allows for both imminence and delay: "But about that day or hour no one knows, not even the angels in heaven, nor the Son, but only the Father" (Mark 13:32; see Matt 24:36). Followers of Jesus need to be prepared for either scenario.

Furthermore, the tension between imminence and delay can also be understood within the framework of the "already"-but-"not-yet" tension. We tend to segregate the two comings of Christ (first at his birth, death, and resurrection, and second at his future return—theologians call these the first and second comings of Christ). But since the first coming of Jesus already inaugurated the end-time kingdom, the second coming will not be some distinct and unrelated event, but the conclusion of what has already

The Gospels

been started—an end times bounded by two comings of Christ, or a coming of Christ split by the period of the end times! With Jesus' incarnation, death, and resurrection, the end had already arrived![43] Therefore, because there were signs that the kingdom had already been inaugurated, it would not be clear if the first followers of Jesus were to expect its consummation immediately or sometime later. The future had already pressed into the present, and changed the way Jesus' followers were to view things. Since the first and second coming of Christ are part of one complex event, Jesus and his followers could expect it could occur within their lifetime, while also expecting the possibility of delay. This would account for statements of Jesus that seemed to promise his return immediately within the lifetime of his followers. This is preferable to concluding that Jesus thought he was going to come back right away but was wrong.

Finally, Jesus' emphasis on the nearness of his coming to consummate the kingdom is not intended to be a prediction of the timing of Christ's return. Jesus is not telling us when he will return. Rather, his emphasis on the nearness of his coming is always to engender vigilance and responsible living in his followers. That is, Jesus' teaching has an ethical urgency to it. Jesus' teaching on his soon return is to motivate responsible and holy living. Since Jesus' disciples do not know when he is going to return, they cannot afford to be lax or lazy, like the unprepared steward in the parable. They must be constantly vigilant since Christ will return at a time that they do not know. In particular, they must demonstrate acts of love and justice to their brothers and sisters who are in need (Matt 25:31–46).

---

43. See König, *Eclipse of Christ in Eschatology*.

3

Acts and Paul's Letters

So Jesus did not say anything that required him to return within the lifetime of his disciples, making a promise that turned out to be mistaken. But what about the rest of the New Testament? There are a number of statements found in Paul's letters that could lead to the conclusion that Paul thought Jesus would return in his lifetime, with the possible implication that Paul, just as it is sometimes claimed for Jesus, was wrong. We will try to understand these statements in their contexts and determine what they might contribute to what we have concluded about the statements made by Jesus in the last chapter. Before examining Paul's letters, in this chapter we will begin by considering how the book of Acts contributes to the issue of the delay of the parousia. However, the bulk of this chapter will be devoted to the letters of Paul.

ACTS

It is not the intention of this treatment of Acts to examine in detail any specific texts that seem to point to a return of Christ within the lifetime of Jesus' followers (the first century). The fact that at Jesus' ascension to heaven (1:9) two angels tell his followers that Jesus will return in the same way that they have seen him taken into heaven may suggest that they thought he could return in their lifetime. Instead, I want to make an observation about the plan and purpose of the book of Acts as a whole, and how it might contribute to our discussion of the problem of the delay of Christ's coming.

The book of Acts, the second volume of Luke's two-volume work, begins right where Luke leaves off. At the conclusion of Luke's Gospel Jesus tells his disciples to wait in Jerusalem for what the Father has promised them, when they will be "clothed with power from on high" (Luke 24:49). In Acts we find that command repeated in 1:5, 8: the disciples are to wait in Jerusalem for what the Father promised them, which is identified as the Holy Spirit. The promise gets fulfilled on the day of Pentecost in Acts 2, and the rest of Acts demonstrates the outworking of this promise of the coming Holy Spirit. Acts 1:8 provides a rough outline for the entire book: "But you will receive power when the Holy Spirit comes on you; and you will be my witnesses in Jerusalem, and in all Judea and Samaria, and to the ends of the earth." The rest of Acts can be seen as unpacking this in that it shows how the Gospel and the promised Holy Spirit spread to lesser and lesser Jewish territories, starting in Jerusalem (Acts 2) and ending in Rome (Acts 28), though it is doubtful that Rome is in itself the final border, the "ends of the earth."[1]

Chapter 1 begins with the disciples asking the risen Lord a question about the coming kingdom promised in the Old Testament. Jesus' mention of the promised Holy Spirit in 1:5 no doubt evoked Old Testament passages in their minds about the coming kingdom of God, which would include the establishment of a new covenant and the pouring out of the Holy Spirit (Isa 44:3; 59:21; Ezek 36:26–27; 37:14; Joel 2:28, which Peter quotes later in Acts 2).[2] Therefore, they ask Jesus if the fulfillment of these Old Testament prophesies is now at hand—will Jesus now restore the kingdom to Israel as promised in these Old Testament texts? Jesus' answer to them is similar to his answer in Matthew 24:36 ("no one knows about that day or hour ... but only the Father")—the timing of this

---

1. Marshall, *Acts*, 61.
2. Keener, *Acts: An Exegetical Commentary*, 682–83.

Where Is the Promise of His Coming?

event is not for them to know: "It is not for you to know the times or dates the Father has set by his own authority" (Acts 1:7). There are at least two ways to understand Jesus' response. First, it is possible that Jesus still expects a future establishment of his kingdom for Israel as promised in Old Testament texts, and the disciples are not to speculate as to the timing. In the meantime the disciples will be Jesus' witnesses. Second, it is possible that the rest of the book of Acts is the way that the restored kingdom will be worked out. Acts 1:8, which is programmatic for the rest of Acts, is shot through with allusions to Old Testament texts from Isaiah.[3] That is, 1:8 could be seen as the way that Isaiah the prophet's promise of restoration and salvation is being fulfilled. It is how the kingdom is going to be restored to Israel as promised in Isaiah and other Old Testament passages, except that gentiles are now included in the one people of God to whom the kingdom is restored. This view does not rule out a future "not yet" establishment of the promised kingdom.

While this latter understanding makes good sense of Acts 1 and the rest of the book, the main point I want to make is that Acts 1:8 and its promise of Spirit-empowered witness that reaches to the "ends of the earth"[4] seems to assume some lapse of time before the return of Christ referred to in 1:10. That is, it assumes a scenario that would not lend itself easily to Christ coming back immediately within the lifetime of his disciples. If the "ends of the earth" in 1:8 simply meant Rome or even some other first-century geographical entity, the book of Acts might not necessarily assume some delay before the return of Christ in order for the gospel to spread to the ends of the earth. However, the reference to the "ends of the earth" probably does not have a specific geographical reference in mind (e.g., Rome, Spain, the inhabited world of that day). Rather it refers primarily to the gentiles who inhabit the entire earth, perhaps represented by Rome,[5] so that this verse has

---

3. Pao, *Acts and the Isaianic New Exodus*, 91–96.

4. This phrase is a direct allusion to Isaiah 49:6: "I will also make you a light for the gentiles, that my salvation may reach to *the ends of the earth.*"

5. Keener, *Acts: An Exegetical Commentary*, 707.

in mind more broadly the gentile mission and their inclusion into the people of God in fulfillment of Isaiah 49:6.[6] Therefore, "Luke's 'ends of the earth,' while prefigured at various stages (including his own conclusion [Rome]), looks beyond the close of his work to the continuing mission."[7]

The upshot of this is that the book of Acts assumes some lapse of time for the followers of Jesus to fulfill the mission of taking the gospel to the "ends of the earth." Jesus certainly was not predicting anything like a two-thousand-year gap! But neither does anything he said in Acts 1 fit an immediate return in his followers' lifetime. Some time (without specifying how much) may be needed for the gospel to go out to all the earth, especially if Jesus (and Luke) envisions it going even beyond the Roman Empire. That is, Acts encourages the ongoing mission to the gentiles, even beyond Rome, a mission that is to continue until Jesus "will come back in the same way you have seen him go into heaven" (1:11). This could be seen, perhaps, as Luke's version of the great commission (Matt 28:18–20).

PAUL' LETTERS

We now turn to Paul's letters. A number of passages from Paul's pen have sometimes been taken to mean that he thought that Christ would indeed return in his (and his readers') lifetime. The implication is that Paul was wrong and later revised his view in light of his impending death (e.g., in Philippians, 2 Timothy). The following treatment is not exhaustive of Paul's teaching on the parousia of Christ, but looks at some of the most relevant and problematic texts.

---

6. Pao, *Acts and the Isaianic New Exodus*, 94–95. The "ends of the earth" in Isaiah 49:6 is in reference to a light for the gentiles.

7. Keener, *Acts: An Exegetical Commentary*, 708.

Where Is the Promise of His Coming?

Romans 13:11–14

> And do this, understanding the present time: The hour has already come for you to wake up from your slumber, because our salvation is nearer now than when we first believed. The night is nearly over; the day is almost here. So let us put aside the deeds of darkness and put on the armor of light. Let us behave decently, as in the daytime, not in carousing and drunkenness, not in sexual immorality and debauchery, not in dissension and jealousy. Rather, clothe yourselves with the Lord Jesus Christ, and do not think about how to gratify the desires of the flesh. (Rom 1:11-14)

In this brief section of Romans 13 Paul uses language that seems to indicate that his readers (and Paul himself) can expect Christ to return immediately, within their lifetime. The "hour" has already come (v. 11), Paul concludes. Their salvation is nearer now than it was at the time they first believed (v. 11). The "night" is nearly passed, and the "day" is ready to dawn (v. 12). It is important to note at the outset that in this section Paul does not speculate on the timing of Christ's coming or how close his readers are to the second coming. The remaining verses in chapters 13–14 make it clear that Paul's main purpose is ethical urgency in his readers. The point is that the readers "should do what Paul has been insisting on in verses 1–10, especially considering the time on the eschatological clock."[8] They are to exhibit behavior fitting to the eschatological situation in which they find themselves.[9] Thus, Paul exhorts his readers to understand the present time, that is, the significance of the present in light of the impending coming of Christ, and to live their lives accordingly, by clothing themselves with Jesus Christ rather than giving into the deeds of the flesh (v. 14).

But what does Paul mean when he says the hour has come, their salvation is now closer than when they first believed, and the night is almost gone and the day is about to dawn? Did Paul

---

8. Witherington III, *Paul's Letter to the Romans*, 317.
9. Moo, *Epistle to the Romans*, 818.

expect Christ to come back immediately, but in his overenthusiasm miscalculated? The term "hour" itself suggests the period of eschatological salvation, which has already been inaugurated by Christ.[10] But *in what sense* is their salvation nearer now than when they first believed the gospel? It is possible that this is a reference to the individual believer's entrance into heaven at the time of death. However, the "salvation" here probably refers to the future consummation of our salvation at the second coming of Christ. It is this eschatological salvation, the culmination of the "hour" that has been inaugurated, that is nearer. This is further explained as the night being almost over and the day about ready to dawn. The "night" stands for this present age, which is almost over, and the "day" stands for the age of salvation that will be ushered in at the second coming of Christ.[11] The language of "nearness" and the night being far along could suggest that Paul thought Christ would come back immediately, but was wrong. But we should probably see this from the same perspective as the texts we will examine below and which we examined in the Gospels: Paul expects that Christ's coming could take place in his lifetime, since the end has already been inaugurated with the first coming of Christ. The end is near in the sense that it is *already pressing in on them*. As Michael Bird suggests, this could be understood as "an intense notion of nearness" on Paul's part.[12] Yet Paul stops short of predicting that the end will definitely come in his lifetime. Richard H. Longenecker sums up Paul's perspective in these verses: Paul "calls on believers in Jesus (1) to recognize this period of time in which they are now living as of great eschatological significance, for it is the time when God is inaugurating 'the age to come' in the 'present existing age,' (2) to realize the implications of living in this time of the overlapping of the 'age to come' and 'this age,' and (3) to think and act responsibly in this epoch of salvation history."[13] The inauguration of the end instills a sense of ethical urgency in Paul's

10. Moo, *Epistle to the Romans*, 822.
11. Kruse, *Paul's Letter to the Romans*, 503-4.
12. Bird, *Romans*, 454.
13. Longenecker, *Epistle to the Romans*, 981.

Where Is the Promise of His Coming?

readers, since the consummation could come at any time. They simply do not know when, which calls for constant vigilance in their daily living.

1 Corinthians 7:25–32

> Now about virgins: I have no command from the Lord, but I give a judgment as one who by the Lord's mercy is trustworthy. Because of the present crisis, I think that it is good for a man to remain as he is. Are you pledged to a woman? Do not seek to be released. Are you free from such a commitment? Do not look for a wife. But if you do marry, you have not sinned; and if a virgin marries, she has not sinned. But those who marry will face many troubles in this life, and I want to spare you this.
>
> What I mean, brothers and sisters, is that the time is short. From now on those who have wives should live as if they do not; those who mourn, as if they did not; those who are happy, as if they were not; those who buy something, as if it were not theirs to keep; those who use the things of the world, as if not engrossed in them. For this world in its present form is passing away.
>
> I would like you to be free from concern. An unmarried man is concerned about the Lord's affairs—how he can please the Lord. (1 Cor 7:25–32)

These words written by Paul to the Corinthian church have often been pointed to as evidence that Paul thought Christ would return immediately. Paul's advice in these verses to both those who are unmarried and those who are married seems to be predicated upon the fact that Paul thinks Christ is going to come back soon, even within his and his readers' lifetime. In verse 26, Paul refers to a "present crisis" (*ten enestosan anagken*) as a reason for singles in the Corinthian church to remain single. He refers to the fact "that the time is short" (v. 29) and "this world in its present form is passing away" (v. 31) as reasons for an apparent neutralizing of the marriage relationship, of emotions, and of material possessions by his first-century Corinthian audience. For example, when Paul tells the Corinthians that because the time is short those who are married should live as if they are not married (v. 29), this would seem odd unless Paul thought Christ was going to return right away. But if this is what Paul had in mind, was he then wrong, since Christ obviously did not come back within Paul's or his readers' lifetimes? Or did Paul have to rethink what he said and change his mind at a later date when it became obvious that Christ might not come back right away? How do we account for Paul's references to "the present crisis," "the time is short," and "this world in its present form is passing away," along with Paul's extreme advice in light of this? It will help for us to unpack in a little more detail the key phrases in this section of 1 Corinthians.

"The present crisis"

"Because of the present crisis, I think it is good for you to remain as you are" (v. 26). What is the "present crisis" that Paul refers to in verse 26? For it is this crisis that motivates Paul to instruct the singles in the Corinthian church to remain single. There are two primary options for understanding the present crisis. First, it is possible that the following verses, vv. 27–31, further elaborate on what the present crisis is; that is, it refers to the parousia (second coming) of Christ.[14] Rather than translating this phrase "present crisis" it could be the "impending crisis." The impending crisis, then, is that "the time is near" (v. 29). Second, the "present crisis" could refer to something that the Corinthians were currently experiencing, such as a famine or persecution.[15] Paul's instructions, then, are for a specific situation that the Corinthian church is facing in the first-century context. According to Andrew Perriman,

> When the community finds itself flying through severe turbulence, it is not the time to go casually walking up and down the aisles of the plane. Passengers are advised to remain seated, with their seatbelts fastened—and in

---

14. Blomberg, *1 Corinthians*, 151–52.
15. Winter, "Secular and Christian Responses to Corinthian Famines," 86–106.

Paul's view frankly, it would be much better if they did not have a husband or wife or children to worry about.[16]

It is difficult to pin the reference down to a specific event, such as a famine, for example, since there is no evidence that Corinth was currently affected by a famine during the time Paul wrote.[17] Yet the word "present" (Greek *enistemi*) usually refers not to something that is about to happen (impending) but something that is already (currently) happening.[18] Therefore, the best suggestion is that it refers generally to the troubles and sufferings that the Corinthians Christians face in this life.[19] Paul's reference to the present crisis may be another way of saying what he has said elsewhere: the lot of Christians is to suffer (see 2 Cor 1:4–7; Phil 1:29–30). Fee nicely captures how this relates to Paul's instructions to the singles to remain single: "Paul seems to be saying, with its suffering and trouble, and in light of the increased troubles that will tend to befall the married (v. 28), the single person will do well to remain that way."[20] But how does this relate to the second coming of Christ? First, we need to examine the remaining expressions.

"The time is short"

Paul further grounds his instructions on marriage in the fact that the "time is short": "What I mean, brothers and sisters, is that the time is short" (v. 29). At first blush this verse could be taken to support the prediction of the imminent return of Christ (within Paul and his readers' lifetime) which turned out to be mistaken. However, this is probably to misunderstand Paul's words here. The "time" that is "short" does indeed refer to the time before the

---

16. Perriman, *Coming of the Son of Man*, 100.
17. Ciampa and Rosner, *First Letter to the Corinthians*, 335–36.
18. Fee, *First Epistle to the Corinthians*, 363–64.
19. Ciampa and Rosner, *First Letter to the Corinthians*, 336–37; Fee, *First Epistle to the Corinthians*, 364–65.
20. Fee, *First Epistle to the Corinthians*, 365.

second coming of Christ and final judgment.[21] But our English translations usually lead us astray here. To say the time is "short" suggests that a quantity of time has already passed, and that there is not much time left until the return of Christ. However, the Greek word translated "short" here, *synestalmenos* in Greek, is a participle meaning "shortened" or "compressed." So Paul is not saying that the time is "short," as if he is concerned with the amount of time we have left (which he miscalculated); rather that time has been shortened or compressed, due to the fact that Christ has already come and inaugurated the end-time. Fee is probably correct that "Paul's concern, therefore, is not with the *amount* of time they have left, but with the radical new perspective the 'foreshortened future' gives one with regard to the present age."[22] That is, "the future, which was set in motion by the event of Christ and the Spirit, has been 'shortened' so that it is now in plain view."[23] Or in the words of David Garland, Paul "is talking not about how little time is left but about how Christ's death and resurrection have changed how Christians should look at the time that is left."[24]

At the same time, there is probably some notion of the time being limited (quantity), since it is shortened or compressed. But this is because the end has already been inaugurated with the first coming of Christ. Because the end has already begun, this means there is limited time until the consummation, without Paul saying how much time is left. The main point is the urgency that now presses upon believers in light of the fact that they live in the end times already. The first coming of Christ, which has inaugurated the end, has shortened or compressed the time, so that God's people of every generation are to live life with this new perspective. Time is not to be seen as continuing as usual and going on indefinitely.

21. Ciampa and Rosner, *First Letter to the Corinthians*, 344.
22. Fee. *First Epistle to the Corinthians*, 374.
23. Fee, *First Epistle to the Corinthians*, 374.
24. Garland, *1 Corinthians*, 328–29. This makes it unlikely that Joseph Plevnik is correct when he says that "As 1 Cor 7:25–31 clearly shows, Paul is convinced that he is living in the last generation on earth" (*Paul and the Parousia*, 158–59). It is probably better to say that Paul is convinced that he *could be* living in the last generation on earth, without Paul predicting that he indeed is.

Where Is the Promise of His Coming?

Here we find the same perspective that we did in the Gospels. Since the end (the kingdom) has already been inaugurated and Christians were already living in the end, the final consummation could come at any time, without demanding that it *has to* come within the lifetime of Paul and his readers. As Paul says in the same letter elsewhere, Christians are those "on whom the culmination of the ages has come" (10:11). That is, the end time of eschatological salvation has already been inaugurated with the first coming of Christ, and "God has begun the process of wrapping up history."[25] The point is that Paul is inculcating eschatological urgency in his readers. The fact that time has been shortened or compressed means that there is an urgency that relativizes all social institutions, including marriage.

This world is passing away

This statement in verse 31 seems to be the implication of the previous statement. Paul now claims that "this world in its present form is passing away" (a similar statement is found in 1 John 2:17 and 2 Peter 3:10; see below on these texts). The implication of the foreshortened or compressed time due to the inauguration of the end with the first coming of Christ, is that the present form of the world is already in the process of passing away.[26] Again, there is no implication of how close the world is to its final dissolution; Paul only tells us that due to the compression of time, the present world is on its way out. Actually, Paul does not say that the world itself is passing away, but the *form* (schema) of the world is passing away. What the form of the world is should be understood in light of the previous verses: the institution of marriage, the present distress in this world, the joys in life. That is, Paul is referring to the social and economic structure of this present world and its experiences.[27] Anthony Thiselton translates it, "For the External structures

---

25. Ciampa and Rosner, *First Letter to the Corinthians*, 465.

26. This seems to be the implication of the present tense form of the Greek verb "passing away" (*paragei*).

27. Ciampa and Rosner, *First Letter to the Corinthians*, 348.

of this world are slipping away."[28] With the first coming of Christ, which inaugurates the end time, and thus compresses the time, this means that the present world and its social and economic structures are in the process of passing away. Once again, Paul's concern is to relativize human institutions, such as marriage, not to plot his temporal existence in relationship to the end.

Summary

Is it possible to say something about the relationship between these three statements by Paul: the present crisis, the shortened time, the form of the world passing away? Though it is difficult to be certain, it seems that Paul is saying that the present distress is part of the shortened or compressed time in which Christians live: a proof that the time has been shortened. Christians should now live with a different perspective on time: it will not go on as usual or indefinitely. A further implication of the shortened time is that the present world structures are already in the process of passing away. At certain times in life, this should at least give Christians pause in pursuing a marriage relationship or placing too much stock in the world's institutions. Thus, while Paul is convinced that the future has already pressed into the present, making the second coming of Christ a reality that should govern their present behavior, nothing Paul says requires the view that the apostle thought that Christ must come back in his and his readers' lifetimes.

1 Thessalonians 4:13—5:11

> Brothers and sisters, we do not want you to be uninformed about those who sleep in death, so that you do not grieve like the rest of mankind, who have no hope. For we believe that Jesus died and rose again, and so we believe that God will bring with Jesus those who have fallen asleep in him. According to the Lord's word, we

---

28. Thiselton, *First Epistle to the Corinthians*, 585.

Where Is the Promise of His Coming?

tell you that we who are still alive, who are left until the coming of the Lord, will certainly not precede those who have fallen asleep. For the Lord himself will come down from heaven, with a loud command, with the voice of the archangel and with the trumpet call of God, and the dead in Christ will rise first. After that, we who are still alive and are left will be caught up together with them in the clouds to meet the Lord in the air. And so we will be with the Lord forever. Therefore, encourage one another with these words.

Now, brothers and sisters, about times and dates we do not need to write to you, for you know very well that the day of the Lord will come like a thief in the night. While people are saying, "Peace and safety," destruction will come on them suddenly, as labor pains on a pregnant woman, and they will not escape.

But you, brothers and sisters, are not in darkness so that this day should surprise you like a thief. You are all children of the light and children of the day. We do not belong to the night or to the darkness. So then, let us not be like others, who are asleep, but let us be awake and sober. For those who sleep, sleep at night, and those who get drunk, get drunk at night. But since we belong to the day, let us be sober, putting on faith and love as a breastplate, and the hope of salvation as a helmet. For God did not appoint us to suffer wrath but to receive salvation through our Lord Jesus Christ. He died for us so that, whether we are awake or asleep, we may live together with him. Therefore, encourage one another and build each other up, just as in fact you are doing. (1 Thess 4:13—5:11)

This passage is the most extended teaching of Paul on the second coming of Christ at the end of history.[29] The purpose of this section is not to examine Paul's eschatology in extended detail or explore

---

29. Some are convinced that Paul is describing a "secret rapture" of the church that is different from and will occur sometime before the second coming of Christ. Due to limitations of space I cannot here offer a defense for my position, but I am convinced that Paul is referring to the second coming of Christ, not a separate secret rapture of the church. See Blomberg, "The Post-tribulationalism of the New Testament."

every phrase in this part of 1 Thessalonians. Rather, I intend to focus on the verses that are germane to the issue addressed in this book. What do these verses tell us about Paul's understanding of the coming of Christ and how this relates to the issue of when he thinks Christ will return? Whatever the precise crisis that Paul is addressing in 1 Thessalonians 4:13-18, it appears that the death of some of those in the Thessalonian church had caused some kind of confusion and grief concerning those who had died. Perhaps the Thessalonians were wondering whether their deceased loved ones would participate in the final physical resurrection.[30] Whatever the case, Paul addresses the Thessalonians with the promise that both those who had died in their midst and those who were still alive would equally participate in the future resurrection at the second coming of Christ (vv. 13-18).

The main contrast in these verses is between what will happen to those who have "fallen asleep" (i.e., those who have died) and those who "remain" (i.e., those who are still alive) at the time of Christ's parousia. It is this latter group, those still alive, that is of interest to us. Twice Paul refers to those who will be alive at the Parousia: "According to the Lord's own word, we tell you that we who are still alive, who are left till the coming of the Lord . . ." (v. 15); "After that, we who are still alive and are left will be caught up together with them in the clouds to meet the Lord in the air" (v. 17). Notice that Paul uses the first person plural "we," which seems to include Paul himself along with his readers, as those who would be alive at Christ's coming. Is Paul claiming that he and his readers would indeed be alive in the day when Christ returns to resurrect his people? Joseph Plevnik concludes from these verses "that Paul himself expects to be alive at the Lord's coming. He also expects that the faithful in Thessalonica to be alive at that time."[31] However, was Paul then mistaken, since Paul and his readers even-

---

30. Beale, *1-2 Thessalonians*, 132-33.

31. Plevnik, *Paul and the Parousia*, 81. Later on Plevnik tempers this comment by saying "the apostle himself hopes to be among those who will live to see the Lord's coming. It is clear that Paul and the Thessalonians live in anticipation of that day" (p. 277).

tually joined "those who have fallen asleep" (v. 15) and nearly two thousand years later we are still awaiting the final resurrection at Christ's coming?

This understanding of Paul's words is unlikely. First, while it is true that later on Paul did wrestle with the fact that he would probably die before the coming of Christ (1 Cor 6:14; 2 Cor 4:14; 5:1; Phil 1:20–24), even here in 1 Thessalonians he recognizes that both he and his readers may die before the coming of Christ. In 5:10, Paul says that "whether we are awake [alive] or asleep [dead], we may live together with him," implying that either could be the case for Paul and his audience. Second, Paul's statement in 4:15 does seem to imply that he thought he and his readers *could* very well be alive at the coming of Christ, without suggesting that Christ *must* return in their lifetime.[32] As Eckhard Schnabel summarizes, "[Paul] reckons with the possibility that he might live to see Jesus returning to earth but does not 'hype' the possibility in terms of a certainty."[33] Third, too much has been made of the first person plural "we." Paul's statement is probably not to be taken too precisely. Paul's primary concern in these verses is to distinguish two different groups and to affirm that both will equally participate in the parousia, not to make a statement about when he thinks Christ will return or to insist that he will be alive when that event occurs. It is even possible that the "we" should be taken very generally, to indicate nothing more than *Christians*, or "anyone who is alive at the coming of Christ" (whenever that event occurs).[34]

Furthermore, since Paul did not know the timing of the parousia, nor the certainty that he would die before it took place, Paul places himself in the only category possible: those who are currently alive. Therefore, Paul at the time of his writing identifies with those who are alive at the time of Christ's return and expresses the possibility that he could be alive when Christ returns (since he has not died yet, and since he does not know when Christ will return).[35]

---

32. Marshall, *1 and 2 Thessalonians*, 127.
33. Schnabel, *40 Questions about the End Times*, 261.
34. Moore, *Parousia in the New Testament*, 109–10.
35. Witherington III, *Jesus, Paul and the End of the World*, 24.

Acts and Paul's Letters

In the words of A. L. Moore, "Paul does not write as one who will certainly be dead at the Parousia but as one who awaits the Parousia as an event which *might* occur at any moment and therefore he reckons with the *possibility* of his being alive at that time."[36] Fourth, in 5:1 Paul appeals to Jesus' "thief in the night" saying, suggesting uncertainty about the timing of the event. Once more, Paul's words imply that Paul could be alive when Christ returns, but he does not predict that Christ must return in his lifetime. Instead, Paul's primary concern is to contrast what will happen to the two different groups, those who have died and those who still alive, at the coming of Christ, and Paul retains the hope that he will be among those who are still alive when Christ returns. As I. Howard Marshall states, "Scholars who insist that Paul's wording *must* mean he expected to be alive at the parousia misinterpret him."[37]

2 Thessalonians 2:1–12

> Concerning the coming of our Lord Jesus Christ and our being gathered to him, we ask you, brothers and sisters, not to become easily unsettled or alarmed by the teaching allegedly from us—whether by a prophecy or by word of mouth or by letter—asserting that the day of the Lord has already come. Don't let anyone deceive you in any way, for that day will not come until the rebellion occurs and the man of lawlessness is revealed, the man doomed to destruction. He will oppose and will exalt himself over everything that is called God or is worshiped, so that he sets himself up in God's temple, proclaiming himself to be God.
>
> Don't you remember that when I was with you I used to tell you these things? And now you know what is holding him back, so that he may be revealed at the proper time. For the secret power of lawlessness is already at work; but the one who now holds it back will continue to do so till he is taken out of the way. And then the lawless one will be revealed, whom the Lord Jesus will overthrow

---

36. Moore, *Parousia in the New Testament*, 118. My italics.
37. Marshall, *1 and 2 Thessalonians*, 127.

Where Is the Promise of His Coming?

with the breath of his mouth and destroy by the splendor of his coming. The coming of the lawless one will be in accordance with how Satan works. He will use all sorts of displays of power through signs and wonders that serve the lie, and all the ways that wickedness deceives those who are perishing. They perish because they refused to love the truth and so be saved. For this reason God sends them a powerful delusion so that they will believe the lie and so that all will be condemned who have not believed the truth but have delighted in wickedness. (2 Thess 2:1–12)

The order in which we find 1 and 2 Thessalonians in our Bible, as well as the titles given to them, most likely suggests the actual chronological order in which Paul wrote these two books. But we can't assume that the order in which books are arranged in the New Testament are the order in which they were written (e.g., most are convinced that of the four Gospels Mark was written first, not Matthew). However, there is good reason to take the order 1 and 2 Thessalonians as reflecting the order in which they were written, and we will proceed with the understanding that 1 and 2 Thessalonians were written in that order.[38] The second letter to the Thessalonians was written in response to a misunderstanding of the "day of the Lord," a term familiar from the Old Testament prophets (Joel 2:11; Zeph 1:7; Zech 14:1) that referred to a time in the future when God would bring about both salvation and judgment and which Paul described in 1 Thessalonians 5:2–6. In other words, it is a term describing the time of the second coming of Christ. It appears that the Thessalonian Christians thought that they were already in the day of the Lord (end-time speculation was already going on in the first century!): "we ask you, brothers and sisters, not to become easily unsettled or alarmed by the teaching allegedly from us—whether by a prophecy or be word of mouth or by letter—asserting that the day of the Lord has already come" (2:1b–2). It is not certain what all contributed to this, but Paul does suggest that some of it was due to alleged previous teaching

---

38. See Blomberg, *From Pentecost to Patmos*, 152–53.

Acts and Paul's Letters

or prophecies by Paul, or to a letter that allegedly was written by him, or perhaps even an overreaction to and misunderstanding of things Paul himself wrote in 1 Thessalonians 4–5.[39] In any case, the Christians in the city of Thessalonica were convinced that they were already living in the final day of the Lord. Paul then writes the letter of 2 Thessalonians in order to dispel the notion that the day of the Lord has already dawned; he writes to convince them that that day has not yet arrived.

The heart of his argument comes in 2:1–12. In this section Paul's logic goes something like this: (1) there are certain things that must happen prior to the day of the Lord; (2) those things have not yet happened; (3) therefore the Thessalonian Christians are not in the day of the Lord. Paul points to at least three things that must take place, but have not yet happened, before the arrival of the day of the Lord.

The first is that "the rebellion" (*apostasia,* from which we get our English word "apostasy") must occur (v. 3). It is not clear exactly what this rebellion is that Paul has in mind. Is it political? Religious? Both? How widespread will it be? There is disagreement as to who will be involved. Will it be Christians, or non-Christians, or both? Who or what will spark it off? We cannot be certain, except that Paul apparently sees a widespread rebellion against God taking place in the end heralding the coming day of the Lord. The idea of a future rebellion was not foreign to earlier Jewish texts. One extra-biblical text, 1 Enoch 93:9, says, "After that in the seventh week an apostate generation will arise; its deeds shall be many, and all of them criminal." It is possible that the rebellion here could more generally refer to "a rebellion" of humanity against God, against order and morals, and an overall increase in wickedness.[40] However, the rebellion could refer to Christians, since Paul himself (1 Tim 4:1) and Jesus (Matt 24:10–12, 24) teach that turning away from the faith will characterize the time before the

---

39. Holmes, *1 & 2 Thessalonians*, 228; Blomberg, *From Pentecost to Patmos*, 153.

40. Holmes, *1 & 2 Thessalonians*, 230; Bruce, *1 & 2 Thessalonians*, 167; see Fee, *First and Second Letters to the Thessalonians*, 281–82.

end. Furthermore, the term *apostasia* is used in the Old Testament (LXX) and the New Testament to refer to religious apostasy.[41] And in Daniel 11:30–45 the prophet envisions an end-time foe attacking the covenant people of God.[42] In this case, Paul envisions a "future massive falling away in the community of faith, the church, throughout the world."[43] However, part of the problem is that in verse 5 Paul reminds the Thessalonians that he has already told them all these things; so presumably he sees no need to repeat everything in detail. One thing is clear, whatever this rebellion is precisely, it has not yet happened, and since it must happen before the day of the Lord can arrive, the Thessalonians can be assured that they are not yet living in that day.

The second sign, probably related to the first one, is the revealing of the Man of Lawlessness (v. 3b). Apparently this Man of Lawlessness will lead the great "rebellion" spoken of above. The fact that this "man" is to be "revealed" (vv. 3, 6, 8) suggests that he had not been revealed yet; so again the Thessalonians cannot be in the day of the Lord. The rest of the passage through verse 12 is a description of what the Man of Lawlessness is going to do and how he will be revealed. First, when he is revealed, he will set himself up as God in God's temple (v. 4). Second, while the power of the lawless one is already at work, it is currently being restrained or held back by someone or something (vv. 6–7). Third, that which is holding the lawless one back will be removed so that the Man of Lawlessness can be revealed (v. 7). Fourth, through the power of Satan this Man of Lawlessness will deceive many with signs and wonders, those upon whom God will send a delusion (vv. 9–11). Fifth, Jesus himself, at his second coming, will destroy the Man of Lawlessness when he is revealed (v. 8).

But what are we to make of all this? The purpose of our discussion is not to provide definitive answers to the interpretation of these "signs"; the purpose is only to show how Paul's teaching here relates to the issue of the delay of the coming of Christ. Before

---

41. Beale, *1–2 Thessalonians*, 203; Green, *Letters to the Thessalonians*, 307.
42. Beale, *1–2 Thessalonians*, 213.
43. Beale, *1–2 Thessalonians*, 207.

we at least touch on what Paul may have had in mind, there are two crucial things we must keep in mind. First, recall again that in verse 5 Paul says he has already taught the Thessalonians about these things, and probably he sees no need to repeat them in detail, "so we are left with a large amount of guesswork."[44] Second, it is difficult to tell how much Paul is using stock apocalyptic language that should not be taken literally, but metaphorically. Thus, is the Man of Lawlessness a literal person (the Antichrist), or metaphorical for the world in rebellion against God or for the power of lawlessness itself? Does the "temple" in verse 4 refer to the literal temple, or is it simply a metaphorical way of highlighting the audacity and arrogance of the Man of Lawlessness: he takes the place of God and demands the worship and allegiance that belongs only to God? This last view has much to be said for it. Further problems arise with the identity of that which is restraining the power of lawlessness (vv. 5–7). Apparently the Thessalonians knew who or what it was (v. 6). There have been numerous explanations given for the identity of the "restrainer" or "what is holding him back," who must be removed so the Man of Lawlessness can be revealed. But we are intruders, trying to make sense of someone else's mail (and written nearly two millennia ago). The following are some (but not all) of the more common proposals, not all of them equally plausible:

1. The Roman government/empire
2. The principle of law and order
3. The proclamation of the gospel
4. The Holy Spirit
5. Satan
6. The archangel Michael (see Dan 10:13, 20–21; 12:1)[45]

With our present limited knowledge it is difficult to be certain, though the restrainer is probably someone/something positive

44. Fee, *First and Second Letters to the Thessalonians*, 285.
45. For this latter suggestion see Pate, *Glory of Adam and the Afflictions of the Righteous*, 308–9.

(rather than evil). We can be certain that the Man of Lawlessness and his deceptive, anti-God activity will be brought to an end with the coming of Christ. And the fact that this Man of Lawlessness is already at work (v. 7) makes it difficult to know when the final, end-time expression has arrived. Regarding the exact identify of these "signs" surveyed above, Gordon Fee suggests that we should take a "Wait and see" attitude.[46] However, even if the precise identify of all these "signs" eludes us, the main point of Paul's argument still stands: Paul is convinced that there are certain things that must take place before the day of the Lord arrives; these things have not yet taken place; therefore, the Thessalonian church can be assured that the day of the Lord has not arrived. Did Paul still think that these things would happen in his lifetime? It is possible that Paul thought that the situation in his own day could escalate in his and his readers' lifetimes so that these things would become a reality and herald the day of the Lord, since Paul says the secret of lawlessness was already at work in his day (v. 7). This is possible. But Paul's only point is that they have not yet happened, and he gives no indication when they will happen or whether they will transpire in his lifetime. According to Ben Witherington III, "A period of time before the End is built into the text of 2 Thessalonians 2."[47] That is, 2 Thessalonians 2:1–12 allows for the possibility of delay before the parousia of Christ (without specifying how long).

We need to conclude by considering how 1 and 2 Thessalonians relate to each other in what they say about eschatology, or the future coming of the Lord. Without requiring that Paul thought the second coming *must* come within his lifetime, 1 Thessalonians certainly seems to suggest that Paul thought it at least *possible* that he and his readers *could* be alive at the parousia; he speaks *as though* he and his readers will be alive at the second coming, although he is speaking rhetorically and his main point is not about the timing of Jesus' return. But in 2 Thessalonians Paul reminds his readers that they are not in the day of the Lord, for certain things must happen, which had not yet happened, before

---

46. Fee, *First and Second Letters to the Thessalonians*, 288.
47. Witherington III, *Jesus, Paul and the End of the World*, 26.

that day arrives. In other words, in these two books we find a balance between the possibility of Christ coming within the lifetime of the readers, but a reminder that certain things that must happen first have not yet happened, a balance between imminence and delay. This perspective is already present in 1 Thessalonians 5, where Paul tells his readers that whether they live or die, they will not be found unprepared, suggesting that Paul did *not* assume that Christ would necessarily come back in the lifetime of his readers even in 1 Thessalonians. Craig Blomberg appropriately entitles his treatment of these two books as "1 Thessalonians: Christ is Coming Soon" and "2 Thessalonians: But Not That Soon!"[48]

To put this all in perspective, 1 and 2 Thessalonians together remind us that we should not think that Christ cannot come back in our lifetime, but neither should we conclude that he necessarily will; certain things have not yet happened. Christ might come back in our lifetime (1 Thessalonians), or there may be some time before events transpire that will herald the coming of the Lord (2 Thessalonians). That is, 2 Thessalonians allows for the possibility of delay. God's people simply do not know and must be prepared for either scenario. Second Thessalonians demonstrates that Paul did not think that Christ would necessarily come in his lifetime, and then was wrong; rather, he reckons with the possibility of a delay. As Eckhard Schnabel sums it up, "Since the final period of history has been inaugurated with Jesus' coming as Israel's Messiah in the first decades of the first century, and since the political situation in Judea was getting worse in the early second half of the first century, the early Christians believed that the end might soon come, uniting them with Jesus Christ and ushering in the last judgment and God's new world."[49] However, Paul stops short of insisting that Christ will indeed come back in his lifetime and refrains from making any predictions, since certain things have not yet happened which must take place before Christ returns.

---

48. Blomberg, *From Pentecost to Patmos*, 139, 151.
49. Schnabel, *40 Questions about the End Times*, 258.

CONCLUSION

In all of the passages that we studied above from Paul's letters, we concluded that none of them justifies seeing Paul as mistakenly predicting that Christ would come back in his and his readers' lifetime. The perspective on the return of Christ in Paul's letters is far more nuanced than that. Instead, we have seen that Paul's statements make far better sense as suggesting that Christ *could* come back within the lifetime of Paul and his readers, since they were already living in the end times, without suggesting that he necessarily will; some texts even allow for a possible delay with the coming of Christ (2 Thessalonians 2).

Paul shares the eschatological perspective of other New Testament authors. Christ's first coming has already inaugurated the end. Therefore, Paul and his readers already live in the end, and see things from that vantage point. The time is now "shortened" or "compressed" (1 Cor 7:25). This means that the consummation to be brought about at Christ's second coming can come about at any time. Again, perhaps it is not helpful to think simply in terms of two separate comings of Christ, but rather the inauguration of the end time, which splits the single coming of Christ into two stages that bring about the end. God's people simply do not know when this process will be completed, and must be prepared for his soon return, as well as a possible delay. God's people cannot live as if Christ will not come back in their lifetime; neither can they life as if he necessarily will. The people of God are called upon to live within the tension of imminence and delay. In addition, the book of Acts at least seems to assume some amount of delay in order for its plan to be put into effect, a plan of a worldwide witness (1:8). The primary purpose for stressing the soon return of Christ is the ethical urgency for godly living, not to predict the nearness of the end.

4

The General Epistles

INTRODUCTION

In the first two chapters of this book we saw that nothing that Jesus or Paul taught demands that they thought Christ would come back in the first century. What about the rest of the New Testament? The purpose of this chapter is to examine a handful of passages found in the section of the New Testament usually designated the "General Epistles" (everything between Paul's letters and Revelation) which have a bearing on the topic of the delay of the coming of Christ. Though not as commonly appealed to as much as the sayings of Jesus or as much as several of the statements of Paul surveyed above (except for 2 Peter 3; see below), there are a few statements in this section of the New Testament that seem to predict the soon return of Christ. One of the classic texts that has a bearing on our topic is 2 Peter 3, where, unlike the other texts we will look at below, Peter responds to the issue of the *delay* of Christ's coming rather than anticipating the soon return of Christ. We will begin below with that text.

Where Is the Promise of His Coming?
2 PETER 3:8–10

> But do not forget this one thing, dear friends: With the Lord a day is like a thousand years, and a thousand years are like a day. The Lord is not slow in keeping his promise, as some understand slowness. He is patient with you, not wanting anyone to perish, but everyone to come to repentance. But the day of the Lord will come like a thief. The heavens will disappear with a roar; the elements will be destroyed by fire, and the earth and everything in it will be laid bare. (2 Pet 3:8–10)

The book of 2 Peter appears to have been written to address the problem of false teachers who were teaching that Christians could cast off moral restraint (particularly sexual) since there is not a coming day of judgment at the second coming of Christ that will hold them accountable (2:1–3, 11–16). If Christ is not going to return to judge, then they can do as they please. The book of 2 Peter is probably a response to several objections by these false teachers as to why they think Christ is not going to return and judge.[1] One of the apparent objections to the coming of Christ which is particularly relevant for our purposes is found in 2 Peter 3:1–4. The objection of the false teachers is summed up in verse 4: "Where is this coming he promised?" The rest of verse 4 explains why these false teachers concluded this: things appear to go on as usual, with no intervention by God in judgment. That is, since God has not intervened yet to judge, it is unlikely that he is going to do so at a second coming of Christ.[2] Unlike some of the passages we examined above from the Gospels and from Paul, the issue here is not the soon return of Christ, but the problem of its delay. "2 Peter 3 contains the most explicit treatment of the delay of the *parousia* in the New Testament."[3]

Verses 5–10 record Peter's response to this objection by the false teachers to Christ's return. Peter's response is in two parts:

---

1. Bauckham, *Jude, 2 Peter*, 154–57.
2. Schreiner, *1,2 Peter, Jude*, 372–74.
3. Bauckham, *Jewish World around the New Testament*, 77.

first in verses 5–7 he argues that God has intervened in the act of creation itself, so he can intervene again into his creation to bring about judgment. The second part of the response is in verses 8–10, which we will focus on in more detail.

Verses 8–9 consists of two statements. First, to the Lord a day is like a thousand years, and a thousand years is like a day. Second, God is not slow in keeping his promises; the apparent "delay" in his coming is due to his kindness and wanting to give humanity an opportunity to repent—if God came back immediately it would mean judgment. What are we to make of Peter's arguments to justify an apparent delay on God's part? And how do they contribute to our understanding of the delay of the parousia of Christ?

The first part of the response contains the well-known statement that comes from Psalm 90:4: "For a thousand years in your sight is like a day that has just gone by." So Peter draws on the words of this psalm to remind his readers that "With the Lord a day is like a thousand years, and a thousand years are like a day" (3:8). How is this a response to the delay that the false teachers were spreading in their teaching? Some have suggested that the comparison of a day to one thousand years (and vice versa) is a statement about God's eternity; it is a statement about the very being of God, that he is outside of time, or even that he does not perceive time sequentially like we do, etc. However, this is probably not how we should understand this statement. The author does not say that a day *is* a thousand years, but that a day *is like* a thousand years to God. New Testament scholar Richard Bauckham has suggested that the force of this statement as it relates to delay is that it "contrasts man's [sic] transience with God's everlastingness, the limited perspective of man whose expectations tend to be bounded by his own brief lifetime with the perspective of the eternal God who surveys the whole of history."[4] Therefore, Peter calls on Christians not to jettison a view of Christ's coming as imminent (see 3:12—the readers are to look forward to the day, and can even speed its coming; see below), but to balance it with "the consideration that the delay which seems so lengthy to [them] may not be so significant within

---

4. Bauckham, *Jewish World around the New Testament*, 81.

that total perspective on the total course of history which God commands."[5] That is, the delay does not seem so significant from the perspective of the Eternal One who sees time and history in its totality, from beginning to end, rather than from the perspective of the typical human span of life (today around eighty years in the USA). What appears prolonged to us is seen as brief from God's perspective.[6] While a delay of seventy to eighty years might seem unbearable to us, the passing of a thousand years is like the passing of a day to God, since he sees the entire span of time. Therefore, human beings, including the false teachers in Peter's day, have no right to judge whether God is unnecessarily delaying.[7]

The next statement gives a rationale for the "delay." Peter explains that God is not slow to keep his promises in the way that some, such as the false teachers of Peter's day, consider slowness and delay. The promises here probably refer to the promise of the parousia of Jesus and all that entails (including the very judgment that the false teachers were denying). The promised return of Christ to judge is indeed coming, so any apparent slowness or delay needs to be understood appropriately. The apparent delay itself reflects God's overall purposes: his mercy and longsuffering in terms of his purpose to allow people to repent (see Exod 34:6).[8] For whenever Christ comes back, it will mean judgment and no further opportunity for repentance. But delay allows for more time for people to turn to Christ in repentance.

This text is of paramount importance for Christopher Hays and others, who see the delay of the parousia as the result of the conditional promise of Christ's coming, where conditions were not sufficiently met (not enough people repented), and so the parousia is delayed. However, (1) Peter is probably not saying that this is the

---

5. Bauckham, *Jewish World around the New Testament*, 81
6. Green, *Jude & 2 Peter*, 326.
7. Davids, *Letters of 2 Peter and Jude*, 277.
8. This mercy and longsuffering is not the reaction of a loving God who is loathe to judge, or who will not judge and only show endless love and mercy. It has a purpose: to get people to repent, so that they can escape the coming judgment. It would be wrong to think that the judgment will be delayed indefinitely.

only or even the paramount reason for delay; (2) Peter is suggesting that delay for the purpose of repentance is *part* of God's overall purpose for delay, not necessarily that an imminent parousia is constantly delayed in response to failure of people to repent, that is, God continuously changes his mind, recalculates and responds to the failure of people to repent by delaying his coming. We should also note the 2 Peter has not given up the hope of a soon return of Christ. Peter shares the perspective of other New Testament authors that the end times have already been inaugurated at the first coming of Christ. Therefore, the presence of scoffers are a sign that the last days have already arrived (3:3). Furthermore, he also encourages his readers in holiness as they wait for the coming of Christ, a text that suggests they could see Christ's return in their lifetime, so they are to wait for it. This is buttressed by Peter's allusion to the "thief in the night" saying of Jesus in 3:10: "But the day of the Lord will come like a thief." In 3:12 they are to "look forward to the day of God" and even "speed its coming." The readers simply do not know when Christ will return; it could be in their lifetime, since they already live in the last days (3:3), yet there could be delay, for which Peter provides an explanation so that his readers do not interpret the delay as indifference or a failure of God's promises that Christ would return. Instead, they should go about living godly lives as they wait for the return of Christ (vv. 11–12).

There is one more statement that we need to deal with. In verse 12 the readers are described as being able to "speed its [the day of the Lord's] coming," most likely by living godly lives in verse 11. At first glance this appears to stand in tension with verses 8–9, where Peter is explaining why the apparent delay—God is giving humanity an opportunity to repent. But now he seems to call on his readers to speed up the day of Christ's coming. This verse seems to be linked with verse 9: Christians are to repent by living godly lives (v. 11). And in this way they can speed up the time when Christ returns. Apparently, then, the coming day of the Lord "is not a fixed date but something that believers can change by their 'holy and godly lives.'"[9]

9. Davids, *Letters of 2 Peter and Jude*, 290.

Where Is the Promise of His Coming?

As strange as this seems to us, most commentators agree that this notion of speeding of the day of the Lord through repentance and godly living has its roots in Jewish literature. In Isaiah 60:22 God is said to hasten the time. This became the basis for other statements in Jewish literature outside of the Old and New Testaments about hastening the time of the end. For example, Sirach 36:7 refers to "hastening the day." In a later Christian text, 2 Clement 12:6 says that "when you do these things [good works], He says, the kingdom of my Father will come." In later rabbinic texts, repentance is said to hasten the end and bring redemption for Israel (e.g., *b. Yoma* 86b; *b. Sanhedrin* 98a).[10] This perspective is probably reflected in the Lord's prayer. "Your name be hallowed, your kingdom come, your will be done, on earth as it is in heaven" (Matt 6:10). Jesus' words seem to suggest that the kingdom comes in response to the prayer of God's people. So 2 Peter 3:12 indicates that by repenting and living holy lives the people of God can speed up the arrival of the day of the Lord. This should not be taken to mean that God does not know the time of his coming, or that he constantly changes his mind as to when he think he will return. But it does suggest that, without overturning God's sovereignty and timing, God takes into account human responsibility. God does choose to respond to human obedience in determining when he will usher in the day of the Lord. As Bauckham concludes, "This does not detract from God's sovereignty in determining the time of the end . . . , but means only that his sovereign determination graciously takes human affairs into account."[11] This is exactly what one would expect to find in a text that is intent on exhorting the readers to holy living in the midst of a corrupt world. Peter emphasizes the responsibility of his readers to godly living as a means of hastening the coming of Christ. Peter does not say that God will continually delay his coming if people do not obey, but he does

---

10. For further discussion of the most important texts see Bauckham, *Jude, 2 Peter*, 325.

11. Bauckham, *Jude, 2 Peter*, 325. See also Schreiner, *1, 2 Peter, Jude*, 390–91.

suggest that human obedience can speed up the time of the coming of Christ.

Second Peter 3, then, provides an important piece of the puzzle in treating the New Testament teaching on the delay of the coming of Christ. Without giving up the perspective of imminence, Peter offers reasons for the delay: (1) God sees the apparent "delay" from the perspective of One who is eternal and views history in its entirety, not from the limited perspective of the brief human life span; (2) the "delay" is part of God's overall purpose, to withhold his judgment and to give humanity an opportunity to repent. In the words of Bauckham, "Against the . . . longing for eschatological righteousness, which the writer clearly shared (3:13), must be set the patience of God who characteristically holds back from condemning the sinner while he may still repent. The believer must hold the two sides in tension. Only God from the perspective of eternity knows the temporal point at which they meet, where the tension will be resolved in the event of the End."[12]

HEBREWS 10:25

> . . . not giving up meeting together, as some are in the habit of doing, but encouraging one another—and all the more as you see the Day approaching. (Heb 10:25)

In order to encourage Christians who may be disheartened by the delay of the coming of Christ, the author of Hebrews (whoever he is), encourages his readers to spiritual vigilance "all the more as you see the Day approaching" (10:25). Though it could be argued that this "Day" refers to the coming of the destruction of Jerusalem in A.D. 70, the day here most likely refers to the parousia, the second coming of Christ, which will be a time of salvation but also of judgment.[13] Although this could be included, this statement by the author suggests more than just "with each passing day the

---

12. Bauckham, *Jewish World around the New Testament*, 82.

13. See Cockerill, *Epistle to the Hebrews*, 481; Koester, *Hebrews*, 446; DeSilva, *Perseverance in Gratitude*, 342; Allen, *Hebrews*, 519–20.

coming of Christ is getting closer"; rather it reflects the perspective found in other places in the New Testament—since the end has already been inaugurated with the death and resurrection of Christ (Heb 1:2), Christians live in a situation of eschatological urgency. The consummation could take place at any time; God's people have always lived on the cusp of the end of history. The end is already pressing in on them. In this case, the perspective of Hebrews 10:25 is very close to that of Romans 13:11–14 considered above. And so here the author warns his readers not to despair or lose heart, but to remain vigilant since the coming of Christ draws near, the time is at hand. In the words of F. F. Bruce, "Each successive Christian generation is called upon to live as the generation of the end-time."[14] As with other biblical texts, the author stops short of insisting that his readers will definitely see the Day in their lifetime, or predicting when it will take place. His main concern is ethical exhortation in light of the eschatological urgency that prevails due to the inauguration of the end with the first coming of Christ.

JAMES 5:7–8

> Be patient, then, brothers and sisters, until the Lord's coming. See how the farmer waits for the land to yield its valuable crop, patiently waiting for the autumn and spring rains. You too, be patient and stand firm, because the Lord's coming is near. (Jas 5:7–8)

In the final chapter of his letter James writes to encourage the poor who are suffering at the hands of the wealthy (5:1–11), by pointing to the parousia of Christ as the point in time at which their injustice will be rectified (5:7–8). Most likely, the scenario is of poor day laborers who work in the fields of the wealthy landowners. The wealthy are oppressing the poor laborers by withholding wages from them and hoarding their wealth. They are to wait patiently for the parousia (v. 8). Therefore, rather than take matters into their

---

14. Bruce, *Epistle to the Hebrews*, 256.

own hands, they should trust in Christ to bring about justice. "The Christians hope, then, is the coming of Christ when all the wrongs suffered will be set right."[15] In verse 7, the readers are encouraged to exhibit patience in the face of economic injustice, which should extend all the way to the parousia ("until the Lord's coming"). In verse 8, this exhortation to patience is supported by a reference to the nearness of the parousia ("the Lord's coming is near"). Both of these statements seem to suggest that James expected that the parousia of Christ would occur within the lifetime of the readers. Scot McKnight takes the language of "nearness" seriously, and then suggests that the coming of the Lord which was near was the destruction of Jerusalem in A.D. 70.[16]

McKnight thinks that the reference to the Lord coming *as judge* in verse 9 tips the scale in favor of this view. However, the second coming itself will be a time of judgment (see 2 Pet 3; Matt 25:31–46), and unlike Jesus' instructions in Matthew 24, there is nothing in the context here that would lead the reader to associate the coming with the events of A.D. 70, so that "James certainly intends, and his readers would certainly have understood, *the Lord's coming* to refer to the return of Jesus as judge and savior."[17] Therefore, we should probably treat these verses no differently that some of Paul's statements that imply the imminence of Christ's return: since Christ has already inaugurated the end times, the consummation at the second coming of Christ could happen at any time. The end is already pressing in on them. Since Christ has already come to inaugurate the end times, his coming to consummate all things could occur at any time. We are to understand James statement that Jesus is "standing at the door" (5:9) to mean that Jesus is temporally near. The readers are to have a new perspective on time: it does not go on as usual but is conditioned by the nearness of Christ's return.

---

15. Davids, *Commentary on James*, 182–83.
16. McKnight, *Letter of James*, 412.
17. Moo, *Letter of James*, 221. Italics his. Moo argues that the term *parousia* virtually came to be used in a technical sense to refer to the return of Christ.

Where Is the Promise of His Coming?

The background for James' statement is Jesus' words in Matthew 24:33: "you know that it [Christ's second coming] is near, right at the door."[18] Therefore, James can speak as if the parousia of Christ could happen at any time, even in his readers' lifetime. Once again, James like other New Testament authors encourages moral diligence (patience) in view of the impending return of Christ to set things right. However, James stops short of insisting that Christ must come back (or predicting that he will come back) in his and his readers' lifetime. Instead, James insists that Christ *could* come back in their lifetime—the readers simply don't know—and like Paul (and Jesus), James appeals to this nearness of the return of Christ in order to motivate his readers to cultivate the virtue of patience. "Every generation of Christians lives (or should live!) with the consciousness that the *parousia* could occur at any time and that one needs to make decisions and choose values based on that realization."[19]

1 PETER 4:7

> The end of all things is near. Therefore be alert and of sober mind so that you may pray. (1 Pet 4:7)

In the midst of a section of exhortation, Peter reminds his readers that "the end of all things is near" as a motivation for godly living. The "all things" that is going to come to an end is the present order of things that will end with the parousia of Christ. Once more, teaching on the return of Christ, whether near or possibly delayed, is appealed to by Peter as a motivation for godly living, not to speculate as to the timing of Christ's return. But what does Peter mean by telling his readers that the end is *near*? Did he expect Christ to come back in his and his readers' lifetime, but then was mistaken in his calculation? Most likely we should take this statement in the same way as James 5:8 above, along with other New Testament texts, which expect the soon return of Christ and the arrival of

18. Blomberg and Kamell, *James*, 235.
19. Moo, *Letter of James*, 224.

his kingdom: since the end has already been inaugurated at the first coming of Christ, the consummation of the "last days" at the second coming could take place at any moment. Peter is operating from the same "compressed time" of the inaugurated end as Paul (1 Cor 7:29). As Peter Davids comments, "This expectation of the imminent inbreaking of God's full and final rule conditions all New Testament teaching."[20]

The author of 1 Peter instills ethical urgency in his readers by reminding them that the end could come at any time; the end is near in that the final arrival of Christ and his kingdom is ready to culminate history at any moment. They already live in the time of the end and must see life from this perspective. Therefore, Peter's readers have no other option but to be alert at all times. As J. Ramsey Michaels concludes, "Peter's meaning is neither that the present age has reached its end nor that the end lies somewhere in the indefinite future. His meaning is that the end will be very soon, although he has no interest in setting dates. There is a time for action, but no time to waste."[21]

1 JOHN 2:18

> Dear children, this is the last hour; and as you have heard that the antichrist is coming, even now many antichrists have come. This is how we know it is the last hour. (1 John 2:18)

In 1 John 2:17 John has just instructed his readers that this present world is passing away: "the world and its desires pass away." Therefore, it is foolish for them to be enamored with the things of this world. But in what sense is the world passing away? The inbreaking of the new era of salvation means that the old era is on its way out. Since the light of the new era has already arrived with the first coming of Christ, the old era characterized by darkness

---

20. Davids, *First Epistle of Peter*, 156.
21. Ramsey Michaels, *1 Peter*, 245.

is already in the process of passing away (2:8).²² This is the characteristic "overlap of the ages" that we have seen elsewhere in the New Testament (the end-time kingdom and salvation has already arrived, even while the present, evil age continues). However, John does not say how long the darkness will take to finally disappear.

In 2:18, John now further reminds his readers that "it is the last hour." While it is once more possible that John thought that he and his readers were living at the very end of history and would see the second coming of Christ to bring history to a close, John's statement must be understood in light of the New Testament conviction that the end has already arrived with the first coming of Christ. Christians were already living in the end ever since the first coming of Christ and his death and resurrection, and since the end had already been inaugurated its consummation could come at any time. Thus, New Testament authors, as John does here, frequently impress upon their readers the urgency of holy living by reminding them that the final wrap-up of God's purposes for the world could happen at any moment, since the process has already begun—they already live in the end and the darkness is in the process of being overtaken.²³ This is what John here calls "the last hour."²⁴ It is not a temporal designation for the final period of history just before the end, but rather a designation of the fact that the "end times" or the "last days" (cf. Heb 1:2) have already arrived with the Christ-event, and the readers now await its consummation (which could happen at any moment). However, John stops short of predicting the end, or suggesting a time table.

CONCLUSION

The section of the New Testament designated the General Epistles has much to contribute to our understanding of the early church's

---

22. In 2:17 the Greek word translated "passing away" (*paragetai*) is in the present tense, which here probably communicates the idea of being in the process of passing away.

23. See Marshall, *Epistles of John*, 148–50.

24. This exact expression occurs only here in the NT.

The General Epistles

perspective on the future parousia of Christ. The authors of these New Testament books share the same eschatological perspective as the rest of the New Testament (Gospels, Paul): with the first coming of Christ the end has already begun. Therefore, the readers live in the end time, the "last days" (Heb 1:2), or the "last hour" (1 John 2:18), designations that refer to the entire period of time between the first and second coming of Christ. Since the end has already been inaugurated, the consummation of all things could occur at any time. Therefore, the writers of the New Testament can stress the urgency of living godly lives since they are already in the end and its wrap-up could occur at any moment. However, these same authors stop far short of predicting that the end will indeed or must take place in the lifetime of the readers, while certainly expecting that it could. One text, without completely abandoning the expectation of the imminent return of Christ, deals with the issue of delay, not by denying it, but by providing a reason for it (2 Pet 3:8–10): delay is only a problem from our (human) limited, finite perspective, and delay is part of God's overall purpose in giving humanity a chance to repent. At least within the broader contours of the canonical General Epistles, delay and imminency-urgency are allowed to sit side-by-side, and God's people must live with this tension. Overall, there is no need to see any of the authors of the New Testament General Epistles predicting the parousia in the lifetime of their readers, but then were found to be in error when Christ did not return. Instead, their statements must be see in light of the eschatological perspective that they share with the rest of the New Testament and in light of their function to provide ethical motivation for the readers. Time will not go one as usual; it is now to be seen in light of the coming of Christ, with the judge standing at the door ready to step through and bring an end to all things.

5

Revelation

INTRODUCTION

As a book that has as one of its main topics "eschatology" (the last things or end times), the very last book of the Bible should play a key role in our discussion of the delay of the parousia. And so we have devoted an entire chapter to this unique book. The book of Revelation is well known for its statements that appear to anticipate the soon return of Christ. The very first sentence of the book begins by claiming that the book will reveal "what must soon take place" (1:1), and a couple verses later promises that the time is "near" (1:3). Likewise, Revelation ends with a promise from Christ, that "I am coming soon" (22:12, 20). Thus, Revelation is bookended with references to the imminent return of Christ. In between these two statements, as we will see below, are other statements that reflect this same perspective of the "soon" return of Christ. How are we to understand these statements? Do they say something different from other New Testament authors? Moreover, as this chapter will attempt to demonstrate, alongside of statements that reflect the imminent return of Christ, there are also clear hints of delay sprinkled throughout Revelation.

Before we jump into the book of Revelation itself, it will be helpful to say something very briefly about the interpretation of Revelation, given the unique kind of book that it is and the

Revelation

difficulties this has caused interpreters. This will provide a perspective for interpreting its statements about the return of Christ. Without getting into the complicated field of "literary genre," how we approach the book of Revelation is influenced to some degree by what kind of literature we think Revelation is. Recent study on the literary type of John's Revelation has suggested that it is a combination of three literary forms: an apocalypse, a prophecy, and a letter.[1] As an apocalypse the book of Revelation records a vision that John had, which is communicated in the form of symbols and images. The content of the book includes visions of heaven and of the readers' present and their future communicated in heavily symbolic form. As an apocalypse it "unveils" the true nature of things so that the readers could have a better understanding of their situation and respond appropriately. Revelation gives us a "behind the scenes" look at history, showing its readers the true and transcendent reality behind earthly happenings. Rome and its Emperor are not in control of history; God is in heaven, seated on his throne and at work to accomplish his plan of redemption through the Lamb (Rev 4–5). Behind the persecuting activity of Rome is Satan's attempt to thwart God's plan (Rev 12–13).

As a prophecy Revelation is not primarily a prediction of future events (*foretelling*), but like Old Testament prophets it is mainly a message to the present day of the readers for encouragement and warning (*forthtelling*). It was meant to address the readers directly with a message relevant to their situation, to call them to maintain their faithfulness to the God of Scripture rather than compromise with the pagan empire of the day (for John and his readers, Rome). And, finally, as a letter, Revelation was addressed to the specific needs of a first-century audience (the seven churches in Rev 2–3) and would have communicated information that they would have understood. Like any of Paul's letters, Revelation was occasioned by specific needs of the first-century churches (see Rev 2–3), and communicated a message that addressed those needs.

---

1. See Mathewson, "Revelation in Recent Genre Criticism," 193–213; Bauckham, *Theology of the Book of Revelation*, 1–22.

Where Is the Promise of His Coming?

The implications of this for interpreting Revelation are that this book, while referring to real persons, places, and events, does not describe them literally, but through symbols and metaphors, much like a political cartoon communicates to its readers today by referring to real present-day political situations, events, and persons, but with graphic, exaggerated images. In other words, Revelation is not to be interpreted "literally" but as a symbolic portrayal of reality. Revelation is also a combination of events that were already taking place in the first century as well as events that lay beyond the horizons of the first readers (e.g., the second coming of Christ and the new creation in chapters 19–22). Furthermore, the book of Revelation would have made sense to the first readers to whom it was addressed. It was not written for some far off generation (e.g., the twenty-first century), but was addressed to seven actual churches in first-century Asia Minor living within the scope of imperial Roman rule. Revelation was written to help its first readers cope with life under imperial Roman rule. Therefore, it would have communicated information that made sense to them and would have addressed their specific needs and situation.

One other feature of the book of Revelation is important for our understanding of this book. John's Revelation ends with an angel commanding him, "Do not seal up the words of the prophecy of this scroll, because the time is near" (22:10). To seal up a scroll would be to keep the contents for a later, future time, and this is exactly what the prophet Daniel is commanded at the end of his book: "roll up and seal the words of the scroll until the time of the end" (12:4). But now John is told just the opposite; with the first coming of Christ "the time is near" (Rev 22:10), fulfillment has already begun, and the contents of Revelation are now being fulfilled, not reserved for some future time and later generation. What this means is not only that Revelation would have been intelligible for the first readers, but Revelation shares the same eschatological perspective as other New Testament books: the end-time prophecies from the Old Testament are already now being fulfilled in and through the person of Christ.[2] Fulfillment has already begun,

---

2. Beale, *Revelation*, 1130.

and the readers now only await the final consummate fulfillment of those promises. Like other New Testament books Revelation shares the perspective that the end-times have already been inaugurated with the first coming of Christ. Jesus has already won the "end-time" victory on the cross (5:5; 12:7–11). Satan has already been defeated. Through his death and resurrection Jesus has already defeated death (1:18). The people of God already constitute a kingdom of priests who rule (1:6; 5:9–10). All that awaits is for the consummated final judgment and new creation (chapters 19–22).

Keeping these observations in mind, in the rest of the chapter we will consider passages in Revelation that have a bearing on our topic of the delay of the parousia of Christ. I will divide these passages into two sections: passages that expect an imminent return of Christ, which seem to expect that the end of history could come within the lifetime of the readers; passages that seem to point to a delay in the arrival of the end of the world. Then we will attempt to synthesize Revelation's teaching on the coming of Christ in light of these texts.

TEXTS THAT SUGGEST "IMMINENCY"

The 'bookends' of Revelation (1:1–3; 22:6–21)

The revelation from Jesus Christ, which God gave him to show his servants what must soon take place. He made it known by sending his angel to his servant John, who testifies to everything he saw—that is, the word of God and the testimony of Jesus Christ. Blessed is the one who reads aloud the words of this prophecy, and blessed are those who hear it and take to heart what is written in it, because the time is near. (Rev 1:1–3)

The angel said to me, "These words are trustworthy and true. The Lord, the God who inspires the prophets, sent his angel to show his servants the things that must soon take place."

"Look, I am coming soon! Blessed is the one who keeps the words of the prophecy written in this scroll."

I, John, am the one who heard and saw these things. And when I had heard and seen them, I fell down to worship at the feet of the angel who had been showing them to me. But he said to me, "Don't do that! I am a fellow servant with you and with your fellow prophets and with all who keep the words of this scroll. Worship God!"

Then he told me, "Do not seal up the words of the prophecy of this scroll, because the time is near. Let the one who does wrong continue to do wrong; let the vile person continue to be vile; let the one who does right continue to do right; and let the holy person continue to be holy."

"Look, I am coming soon! My reward is with me, and I will give to each person according to what they have done. I am the Alpha and the Omega, the First and the Last, the Beginning and the End.

"Blessed are those who wash their robes, that they may have the right to the tree of life and may go through the gates into the city. Outside are the dogs, those who practice magic arts, the sexually immoral, the murderers, the idolaters and everyone who loves and practices falsehood.

"I, Jesus, have sent my angel to give you this testimony for the churches. I am the Root and the Offspring of David, and the bright Morning Star."

The Spirit and the bride say, "Come!" And let the one who hears say, "Come!" Let the one who is thirsty come; and let the one who wishes take the free gift of the water of life.

I warn everyone who hears the words of the prophecy of this scroll: If anyone adds anything to them, God will add to that person the plagues described in this scroll. And if anyone takes words away from this scroll of prophecy, God will take away from that person any share in the tree of life and in the Holy City, which are described in this scroll.

He who testifies to these things says, "Yes, I am coming soon." Amen. Come, Lord Jesus.

Revelation

The grace of the Lord Jesus be with God's people. Amen. (Rev 22:6–21)

There are a number of texts in Revelation that seem to point to the soon return of Christ, such that they could be taken to mean that Christ will surely come back within the lifetime of the author John and his readers. As we already noted, the most important texts are those that bookend Revelation: 1:1; 22:7, 10, 12, 20. Several verses, 22:7, 12, 20 promise that fulfillment of the events in Revelation, including the coming of Christ at the end of history, will take place "soon." 1:3 and 22:10 also add that "the time is near." The events that are "near" are probably all of the events depicted in Revelation, including the parousia. Much of Revelation's vison was already being fulfilled in the first century in the church's struggle with the Roman Empire. So, for example, Revelation 12–13 serve to explain the true source of the struggle that the churches in chapters 2–3 face, with the Roman Empire portrayed as a hideous seven-headed beast. But the events in Revelation clearly include the second coming of Christ (see especially Rev 19–20). But in what sense will the parousia take place *soon* and in what sense is the time *near*, since we still await its fulfillment nearly two thousand years later?

One could argue once more that John the Seer thought that Christ was going to come back within his and his readers' lifetime, but was simply mistaken. John wrongly predicted that he and his readers would be alive when Christ returned. Some have tried to alleviate this problem by taking the references here to "soon" and "near," along with other apparent expressions of imminence throughout Revelation, as references to the destruction of Jerusalem in A.D. 70.[3] This event indeed would have qualified as "soon" or "near" for the author and readers of Revelation.[4] This view, that most if not all of Revelation refers to events that have already transpired in the first century and the destruction of Jerusalem

---

3. Chilton, *Days of Vengeance*, 51–52.

4. This view also depends on dating Revelation before the destruction of Jerusalem in A.D. 70, perhaps in the mid-60s. Most scholars, however, are of the opinion that Revelation was written after the destruction of Jerusalem.

Where Is the Promise of His Coming?

(known as the *preterist* view of Revelation),[5] can be commended in making Revelation relevant to the first-century readers for whom it was written, rather than seeing it as a prediction of events that lie far off in the distant (twenty-first century) future. However, though this is not the place for a detailed critique of this way of reading Revelation, there are too many sections that simply make better sense as referring to the second coming of Christ at the end of history. And so we are back to the tension: how are these events promised in Revelation, especially the second coming of Christ, to be regarded as "soon"?

Another possible way to solve the problem is by understanding the Greek word *tachu* that is usually translated "soon" instead as meaning "suddenly" or "quickly," referring to the speed or rapidity at which the events will be fulfilled whenever they begin fulfillment.[6] Therefore, John was not predicting that the end would come anytime soon, but that whenever it did come it would happen quickly and speedily. While this is a possible meaning the Greek word *tachu*, it is probably not the meaning here. At the end of the book Jesus promises to come "soon" or "quickly." The opposite of "quickly" would be "slowly." It is doubtful that Jesus is emphasizing that when he returns it will transpire quickly rather than in a slower manner. It does make good sense to see John emphasizing that Jesus could come soon, rather than there being a delay.[7] Also, taking the word *tachu* to mean "quickly" still does not solve the problem of John saying that certain events are "near." Therefore, we should probably understand these statements in a similar way to the references to the time being "near" (1:3; 22:10). Those translations that render this word as "soon" are correct (e.g., NIV 2011). Again, this refers to all the events depicted in Revelation; many of them were near from the standpoint of being on the verge of or already beginning fulfillment in the persecution of the church in Asia Minor (1:4) at the hands of the Roman Empire. But these events that are near must also include the parousia, the end.

---

5. See Gentry Jr., "A Preterist View of Revelation," 37–92.
6. Walvoord, *Revelation of Jesus Christ*, 35.
7. Schnabel, *40 Questions about the End Times*, 259.

These events, especially the end, will come soon or without delay.[8] Again, John sees all of this as one complex of "end time" events that are now being fulfilled in Christ. In other words, we should see the coming of Christ in the same way as some of the references in the Gospels and elsewhere in the New Testament (treated above), where the authors anticipate the soon return of Christ, without insisting that it *must* take place in their lifetime (see Mark 13:29, 33; Matt 24:33, 44; 1 Cor 7:29; Jas 5:8; Heb 10:25).

Since the end has already been inaugurated with the first coming of Christ, the end time is already present and can reach its consummation at any time. Hence, Jesus and his followers expected the consummation of the kingdom with the second coming of Christ to occur at any moment, to be near or at hand, without insisting that it had to take place immediately. Likewise, John instills in his readers an urgent expectation of the end in order to motivate them to holy living in the midst of the pagan environment in which they lived. But he stops short of predicting when the end will come, and as we will see below, delay is just as much a part of Revelation's message as is the soon return of Christ. Like Jesus and the apostles, John's primary purpose is exhortation, not to speculate on the timing of Christ's return. He writes to warn his readers of the danger of accommodation with their pagan surroundings, and urges them to faithful witness to the end (2:10; 12:10). John does this by appealing to expectation of the soon return of Christ, lest his readers be caught unprepared should Christ return in their lifetime. In other words, John's insistence that the end is near has a hortatory appeal and urgency.

The messages to the seven churches (2:16; 3:11)

> Repent therefore! Otherwise, I will soon come to you and will fight against them with the sword of my mouth. (Rev 2:16)

---

8. Bauer, Danker, Arndt, and Gingrich, *Greek English Lexicon*, 993.

Where Is the Promise of His Coming?

> I am coming soon. Hold on to what you have, so that no one will take your crown. (Rev 3:11)

The seven "letters" to the churches (chapters 2–3) are actually seven prophetic messages addressed to seven historical churches located in important cities in ancient Asia Minor for the purpose of comforting but mainly warning them. Like the statements at the beginning and end of Revelation, at least twice in the "letters" Christ promises that he is coming *soon*: "Repent therefore! Otherwise *I will soon come* to you and with fight against them with the sword of my mouth" (2:16); "*I am coming soon*. Hold on to what you have, so that no one will take away your crown" (3:11). Gregory Beale has argued that these references to Christ's coming in chapters 2–3 are conditional references to the coming of Christ in history to judge the churches, though they could include a reference to the second coming of Christ at the end of history as well. "Christ's 'coming' . . . in the Apocalypse is understood better as a process occurring throughout history; the so-called 'second coming' is actually a final coming concluding the whole process of comings."[9]

However, the references to coming soon in 2:16 and 3:11 reflect the language of Jesus' promise to come soon at the end of the book in 22:7, 12, 20, the latter of which are clear references to the second coming of Christ. Of the two verses, 2:16 seems most clearly to refer to the possibility of a temporal judgment in history of the church of Pergamum. The reference to the sword coming of the Christ's mouth in 2:16 also reflects the language of 19:15, 21, which refers to Christ defeating his enemies *at his second coming*. However, here in 2:16 the emphasis is on the inauguration of that end-time judgment in the temporal judgment of the church at Pergamum. Grant Osborne writes of 2:16 that "this 'coming' refers both to the present judgment upon the church and to the final judgment at the 'parousia.'"[10] Therefore, this verse could refer to

---

9. Beale, *Revelation*, 198.
10. Osborne. *Revelation*, 146.

the coming of Christ to historical Pergamum for the purpose of their judgment.

The promise of Christ's coming in 3:11 ("I am coming soon") seems to reflect even more clearly the perspective of 22:7, 12, 20, where the promise of Christ's coming refers to his second coming. There is no need to see in 3:11 an inaugurated fulfillment in history. The promises of Christ coming soon in 3:11 should be understood in the same way as these other references: as an indication of the imminent expectation of the return of Christ at the end of history, which John shares with other New Testament authors. Again, John stops short of predicting that Christ will indeed return within his and his readers' lifetime, but urges his readers of the need for steadfastness and repentance by reminding them of the possibility that Christ might return in their lifetime. Because Christ has already inaugurated the end times with his first coming, the second coming, which will bring the end times to their consummation, can happen at any moment. Time takes on a different shape with the first coming of Christ and the inauguration of the end times. So John's readers must be prepared.

In three other places in the messages to the churches, Jesus refers to his "coming" to the readers of Revelation in those churches. In 2:5 Christ's coming seems specifically to be in judgment against the church in Ephesus, conditioned upon whether they repent or not. Revelation 2:25 encourages the church in Thyatira to "hold on to what you have until I come."[11] Unlike verse 5, this coming is not restricted to the specific historical situation of the church (e.g., removing their lampstand). This is further explained in the next verse: "until Christ comes" is the "end" mentioned in verse 26. The reason the readers should hold on until Christ comes is that he will reward them at his second coming with the authority to sit with him on his throne (v. 27, a promise fulfilled in 20:4–6, and 22:1–5). So this is another exhortation to the church to be faithful

---

11. The word for "come" in this verse is different from the word used in the other verse. Here it is the Greek word *heko*, whereas the other verses use *erchomai*.

Where Is the Promise of His Coming?

in light of the second coming of Christ, though John does not use the language of "soon" here.

The final verse relating to Christ's coming in 3:3 uses the "thief in the night" language that goes back to Jesus' own teaching in the Gospels about his second coming (Matt 24:43; Luke 12:39). This "thief in the night" saying of Jesus also lies behind a statement by Paul in 1 Thessalonians 5:2–4, and a statement by Peter in 2 Peter 3:10. In both of these places the thief saying refers to Jesus' second coming. It is used in one other place in Revelation to also refer to the second coming of Christ, in Revelation 16:15. A very common way of taking 3:3, however, is to see it as another conditional judgment that would come specifically on the church in Sardis in history if they fail to repent.[12]

However, I would argue that the reference here is to the second coming: the fact that the "thief in the night" saying is used in all the other references in the New Testament, including the only other one in Revelation (16:15), to refer to the second coming of Christ[13] suggests that this is the case here in 3:3 as well. Furthermore, what is conditional upon their repentance is not whether Christ comes to them or not, but whether his coming will take them by surprise or not. This is how the image is used in 1 Thessalonians 5:2–4—the parousia of Christ will have a different effect on those who are prepared and those who are not. Here in 3:3 we find something similar: the parousia of Christ will have a menacing effect on those in the church at Sardis who are not prepared for it: it will catch them unaware, like a thief![14] But the second coming did not take place in the lifetime of the church at Sardis! Yet we should understand 3:3, and 2:25, in the same way as the other references to Christ coming soon in Revelation—Christ could come within their lifetime (without John insisting that he must). As long as the Christians in Sardis are alive, Christ coming in their lifetime is a real possibility. Since Christ's coming is imminent, the Christians

---

12. Beale, *Revelation*, 275–76; Mounce, *Revelation*, 111–12; Osborne, *Revelation*, 178; Smalley, *Revelation to John*, 83.

13. Koester, *Revelation*, 313.

14. Bauckham, *Climax of Prophecy*, 104.

in Sardis are warned to repent lest the second coming catches them off guard, like a thief, just as with the Thessalonian Christians in 1 Thessalonians 5:2–4. Likewise, the reward of ruling at the second coming is held out to the church in Thyatira as a motivation for holding on to the end (2:25).

The seven heads of the beast (17:9–11)

> This calls for a mind with wisdom. The seven heads are seven hills on which the woman sits. They are also seven kings. Five have fallen, one is, the other has not yet come; but when he does come he must remain for a little while. The beast who once was, and now is not, is an eighth king. He belongs to the seven and is going to his destruction. (Rev 17:9–11)

In Revelation 17, John sees a vision of a woman riding upon a beast. The beast is described in some detail, including the feature of having seven heads and ten horns. What is unique about chapter 17 is that it is one of the only places in John's Apocalypse where one of his visions is interpreted for him by an angel. Yet as we will see, the interpretation by the angel is almost as confusing for interpreters today as the vision itself! The interpretation of the vision is recorded in verses 8–18. The section of the interpreted vision that we want to focus on is the explanation of the beast's seven heads, which is found in verses 9–11, quoted above.

The seven heads actually get a dual interpretation. First, they are identified as seven mountains upon which the woman sits, no doubt an allusion to the ancient city of Rome, known in antiquity as the city on seven hills.[15] But second, the seven heads also represent seven kings or rulers, no doubt a reference to Roman emperors who ruled over the Roman Empire. To be more specific, the angel tells John that five of the rulers have already fallen, one is, and there is one still coming, totaling seven.

---

15. Osborne, *Revelation*, 617.

Where Is the Promise of His Coming?

There has been much speculation on the identity of these seven Roman emperors historically. Presumably, one could date precisely the book of Revelation if one could figure out which emperor the statement "one is" refers to. Part of the problem is, no one can agree where to start counting the seven heads—with Julius Caesar, or Caesar Augustus, or someone else? And do we include the three emperors who ruled only very briefly over a year's period of time (Galba, Otho, Vitellius)?[16] However, it is more likely that the number seven is meant to be symbolic, as this number is elsewhere in the book of Revelation. It refers to the complete number of Roman emperors and totality of Roman power, rather than seven specific historical Roman rulers.[17] Therefore, there is no need to identify which are the five historical rulers who have fallen, and which is the one that is currently ruling (though presumably the first readers knew who they were living under!), so that we might know who the "one who is not yet" is. So what is the effect of saying that of the complete number of rulers, five have already fallen, one is, and there is still one to come?

By saying that five have fallen, one is, and one is still to come (v. 10), it sounds as if John thinks that the time is short and the end is going to come very soon; after all, the readers would be living under the one that "is" (whomever that might be; Domitian?), and there is only one other ruler left "who has not yet come," indicating a short period of time in comparison to the reign of the five that have already fallen. The point? Much of history has already run its course. Now there is apparently only a short time before the last ruler, the one who is to come, emerges, and he himself will only reign for a "brief time." So apparently there is only a short time left for John and his readers before Christ comes to bring an end to things. But then John also describes an eighth which is the beast himself. What are we to make of this? Did John predict that Christ would come within some of the readers' lifetime after a succession of Roman emperors, only to be wrong? And who is the eighth one that emerges in verse 11? Is this another emperor? Perhaps we can

---

16. Aune, *Revelation 17–22*, 946–47.
17. Mounce, *Revelation*, 315; Aune, *Revelation 17–22*, 948.

Revelation

be excused for being a little baffled at all this, since John himself recognizes the need for wisdom to understand it (v. 9)!

As we have already seen, the seven heads represent or symbolize the complete and total power of godless, evil, oppressive Rome, not a specific number of emperors. But John is still locating himself and his readers within the overall succession of Roman Emperors. The effect of placing the readers during the time of the sixth emperor (the one who is) with only one more to come, is to show the nearness of the end. Symbolically, Roman rule has run its course, with little time remaining after the current ruler (the one who "is"); a symbolic seventh will emerge for a brief time. The Greek word translated a "short time" or "little while" (*oligon*) is the same word used of Satan in 12:12 who has been cast out of heaven and is permitted to wreak havoc on the church for a brief time. However, this "short time" extends from Satan's being cast out of heaven at the death and resurrection of Christ until the second coming of Christ when he is destroyed (20:1–15). The word itself suggests that there could be some delay. In other words, the "short time" or "little while" of the seventh head, like the time of Satan's wrath, could also last for a while temporally, until Christ returns. There is no way of knowing when it will come to an end. John's point is only to show that earthly, pagan rule (which for the first readers was in the form of the Roman Empire) will not last forever. Roman rule is living on borrowed time, and it will come to an end.

What about the beast who is an eighth (v. 11)? It is doubtful that John is envisioning an eighth ruler who will temporally follow the seven. Rather, the beast seems to coincide with the seven heads (which in fact all belong to the beast!). He is greater than any of the heads and works his evil in all of them.[18] But as the text tells us, his fate is sealed—he is going to destruction! "Eighth" is important because it tells us about the identity of the beast. He transcends all of the seven heads and stands behind them, but also it may that eight is a triangular number related to 666, or eight may recall the "eighth" day of creation and the resurrection of Christ on the eighth day, so that the beast is once more seen as mimicking

---

18. Kistemaker, *Revelation*, 473.

Christ in his resurrection, but falls far short.[19] The main point is that the beast, which lies behind the Roman emperors (and any other regime that arrogates divine power) is going to destruction, a reference to the parousia (second coming) of Christ.

Admittedly, this text in John's Apocalypse is difficult to figure out, and we should probably be cautious about forming any dogmatic conclusions about it, and admit a fair degree of uncertainty (and humility!). However, one thing we can conclude is that it does appear that John's language about the seven rulers is another way of stressing the nearness of the end and of Christ's coming, which has been emphasized through the book ("I am coming soon"). There is only a short time before the succession of Roman rulers, and therefore world history, runs its course, and the beast makes its final appearance to war against the Lamb. The end is near because Jesus has already inaugurated the kingdom, judged Satan, and brought end-time salvation to his people, in advance of the final emergence of the kingdom at his second coming. As we have already seen, this does not mean that John was mistakenly predicting that the end would come within his lifetime or immediately after the last Roman emperor. It only means that since the end was already inaugurated by Christ at his first coming, the readers are already living in the end, and earthly rulers are living on borrowed time. The wrap up of the end-times can come at any time, without John telling us exactly when. So by placing the readers at the sixth ruler, with only one more to come for a short time, John message is to emphasize the nearness of the coming of Christ and that his coming will mean the end of earthly empires, without predicting exactly when it will happen. Therefore, the readers should resist the temptation to associate with pagan Rome, since it is on its way out. There is still enough ambiguity (the length of the "short time," the reference to an "eighth" which transcends the seven) that it is impossible to tell how long until the end arrives. "The important point is that the end is drawing near."[20] And John's main point is to show that the power behind the Roman Empire and its evil pre-

---

19. Beale, *Revelation*, 875–76.
20. Mounce, *Revelation*, 316.

decessors is bound for judgment. So the church must adjust their eschatological clocks and resist following it.

TEXTS THAT SUGGEST "DELAY"

As we have already noted in passing, the book of Revelation does not only insist on the nearness of the return of Jesus Christ at the end of history. Statements of "soon" and imminence within the book are balanced by indications of delay. This element of delay can be found in specific texts, but as we will see also it is embedded within the very structure of the book of Revelation itself. Statements of delay serve to balance out statements of imminency within Revelation.

Wait a little longer (6:9–11)

> When he opened the fifth seal, I saw under the altar the souls of those who had been slain because of the testimony they had maintained. They called out in a loud voice, "How long, O Sovereign Lord, holy and true, until you judge the inhabitants of the earth and avenge our blood?" Then each of them was given a white robe, and they were told to wait a little longer, until the number of their fellow servants and brothers were to be killed as they had been was completed. (Rev 6:9–11)

Probably the primary text that suggests delay in Revelation is the account of the fifth seal in Revelation 6:9–11. With the first round of initial (seal) judgments on the world, following a vision of four horses and their corresponding judgments, with the fifth seal John sees a vision of souls under the altar; they are there because they have been executed for their testimony to Jesus.

Their initial cry, "How long, O Sovereign Lord . . . until you judge the inhabitants of the earth and avenge our blood" (v. 10), suggests a desire for (and confidence in) the imminent return of

Christ to right the wrongs done to them.[21] The cry "How long!" is found in numerous places in the Old Testament as a response to God's apparent lack of intervention and delay (Pss 6:3; 13:1–2; 74:10; 79:5; 80:4; 89:46; 90:13; 94:3; Jer 12:4; Hab 1:2).[22] Now the saints in John's vision echo the same cry in response to God's apparent lack of action on their behalf. However, the response to their cry is one that suggests even further delay: "then each of them was given a white robe, and they were told to wait a little longer, until the number of their fellow servants and brothers who were to be killed as they had been was completed" (v. 11).

There is actually both imminence and delay in this response. First, the response indicates that God will, indeed must, vindicate the cause of the martyrs. Second, the amount of time they are to wait for vindication is specified as "a little while" (Greek: *chronon micron*). At the same time, this statement indicates that there will indeed be *delay* in the form of a period of time before vindication comes; it will not take place immediately. It calls for the saints to be patient: "The exhortation to rest means that the saints in heaven are to be patient in that desire for God to answer their request."[23]

Delay is also indicated by the image of the completion of the number of martyrs before vindication comes. This notion of a predetermined number of those who will die waiting to be completed before the end comes is not unique to John, but is found in other extra-biblical apocalyptic texts from around this period (1 Enoch 47:1–4; 4 Ezra 4:35–37; 2 Baruch 23:4–5).[24] In 4 Ezra 4:35–37, the righteous who have been put to death ask "How long are we to remain here?" Then an angel answers, "When the number of those like yourself is completed." John is unique in that it is the number of *martyrs* waiting to be completed.[25] Whether he thinks there is actually a specific number of saints yet to die for their faith, or is

---

21. The cry "how long" at least suggests that the suffering has gone on longer than expected without adequate vindication.
22. Bauckham, *Climax of Prophecy*, 51.
23. Beale, *Revelation*, 394.
24. Bauckham, *Climax of Prophecy*, 48–56.
25. Bauckham, *Climax of Prophecy*, 52.

only using a standard, familiar apocalyptic theme, John integrates this image into his account of his own vision in order to provide an explanation for the delay: there will be further time for the church to carry out its faithful witness, even in the face of martyrdom. God will indeed vindicate his people of the evil they have suffered; but before that there will be a time of the church's faithful witness in the midst of suffering and persecution. Again, John's theme of delay has an exhortational purpose: to motivate God's people to patiently persevere in their faithful witness in the face of persecution until the end, not to predict how long this period of time will last. "The *assurance* that God will unquestionably punish the evil world becomes a motivation for Christians to persevere in their witness through suffering on earth."[26]

The end that never comes: the literary shape of Revelation

One feature of Revelation that is built into its very literary structure is that the author brings the reader to the very brink of the end throughout the book, but then backs off again and again so that the end seems to never quite arrive. In the words of David Barr, when we read Revelation "we wait for an end that never comes."[27] That is, the reader experiences delay after delay while reading the account of John's vision "as the End is constantly approached but not definitively reached."[28] In Revelation 5, the Lamb receives a scroll with seven seals; the scroll probably contains God's plan for establishing his kingdom on earth as it is in heaven. So one would naturally expect after chapter 5 a rather straightforward progression in the unfolding of God's plan to bring about redemption. But this expectation is frustrated over and over again in reading Revelation.[29] Instead, there are stops and starts, progress but delay. For example, as we have already noted above, in the sequence of

---

26. Beale, *Revelation*, 394.
27. Barr, "Waiting for the End That Never Comes," 105.
28. Bauckham, *Theology of the Book of Revelation*, 157.
29. Bauckham, *Jewish World around the New Testament*, 84.

Where Is the Promise of His Coming?

seals in chapter 6 (see above), the sequence is slowed down with the question from the souls below the altar: How long, O Lord? The judgments seem to come to a halt or to be put on hold. The sixth seal then appears to bring us to the end, the second coming of Christ.

> I watched as he opened the sixth seal. There was a great earthquake. The sun turned black like sackcloth made of goat hair, the whole moon turned blood red, and the stars in the sky fell to earth, as figs drop from a fig tree when shaken by a strong wind. The heavens receded like a scroll being rolled up, and every mountain and island was removed from its place. Then the kings of the earth, the princes, the generals, the rich, the mighty, and everyone else, both slave and free, hid in caves and among the rocks in the mountains. They called out to the mountains and the rocks, "Fall on us and hide us from the face of him who sits on the throne and from the wrath of the Lamb! For the great day of their wrath has come, and who can withstand it." (Rev 6:12–17)

The reader might expect a grand conclusion to the narrative at this point. The great day of God's (and the Lamb's) wrath has arrived. But there is no narration of what happens at the arrival of this day, and the reader is left hanging. Furthermore, the scroll has seven seals (5:1–2), but chapter 6 only unseals six of them, so we wait for the seventh. Yet the reader's expectations are again frustrated. The seventh seal is delayed until Revelation 8:1. And there is a further intervening scene in chapter 7, which itself marks delay: judgment is withheld until the faithful (144,000) are sealed. The seventh seal is finally opened in 8:1, but then there is only silence in heaven, and no narrative of the end! Instead, what follows in chapters 8–9 is another sequence of judgments in the form of trumpets. The judgments proceed rather slowly, especially with the fifth and sixth trumpet in chapter 9, which take up about as much space as the first four (chapter 8). Verse 2 clearly leads us to believe that there will be seven of them: seven trumpets are given to seven angels. Yet once again, chapter 9 only takes us through to the sixth trumpet, and the reader's expectation of a seventh trumpet is again

Revelation

frustrated, and the end is once more delayed. Instead of the seventh trumpet one finds a lengthy intervening section in chapters 10–11 consisting of an angel giving a scroll (the same one from chapter 5?) to John and commissioning him to prophesy, followed by an account of the measuring of a temple and the ministry of two witnesses in chapter 11.

In 10:7 the angel announces that there will be no more delay and that all would be fulfilled at the seventh trumpet. But there is yet further delay with the account of the measuring of the temple and the ministry of the two witnesses in 11:1–13. There is more delay, as these verses recount a length of time (forty-two months) for the church's witness.[30] The seventh trumpet is finally blown in 11:15. But what follows is not a narration of the end, but two speeches by the angel (v. 15) and the twenty-four elders (vv. 16–18), which announce the arrival of the kingdom. Verse 19 ends with the heavenly temple being opened and a display of thunder and lightning, leaving the reader expecting a narration of the final arrival of the kingdom. But once again the reader's expectation is frustrated. Rather than the end, there is another intervening section in chapters 12–13 that narrates the source of the struggle that the people of God face in this life: Satan (chapter 12) and his two beastly cohorts (chapter 13). Both visions bring the reader back to this present world. Even when Satan is judged and cast out of heaven, this judgment is apparently not final, because he still has time (albeit a "short time") to wreak havoc on the people of God (12:12).

The reader's expectation of the end is rejuvenated with another series of seven judgments in the form of seven bowls in chapter 16. The bowl judgments are narrated in fairly quick succession, and all seven are narrated in chapter 16. But with the sixth bowl (vv. 12–14) the kings are gathered for the battle of Armageddon, but the battle is never described. With the seventh bowl we hear the voice, "It is done!" and judgment is poured out on Babylon and

---

30. Like most commentators, I understand the two witnesses to symbolically represent the entire witnessing church. See Bauckham, *Theology of the Book of Revelation*, 84–88.

all humanity. The story then continues with the lengthy account of Babylon's judgment (chapters 17–18) followed by a transitional section of removal scenes in 19:11—20:15, where everything is judged (humanity, the two beasts, Satan, and finally everything at the Great White Throne Judgment). Even Satan's judgment (20:1–10) evokes delay: he is bound for a thousand years, but then is let out again for a "short time" (20:3) to assemble an army for yet another, final battle![31] Once more, the end is delayed, if only briefly.

Then the end *finally* comes! The end-time new creation (21:1—22:5), anticipated in Revelation but constantly deferred, finally arrives. But only after several stops and starts, progressions and delays! All of this has the effect of creating a sense of delay for the reader, "as the End is constantly approached, not definitively reached."[32] This literary effect of delay corresponds to the theological tension between imminence and delay. It reminds the attentive reader that the end is just around the corner, but just when the reader rounds the corner he/she may find that the end has been pushed just out of reach—it has been delayed. Christ could come back "soon," but there could be a delay until he arrives. The audience of Revelation must be prepared for either, and in the meantime maintain their faithful witness for Christ even in the face of persecution (chapter 11).

CONCLUSION

In this chapter we have observed that Revelation shares the same tension between the soon return of Christ and the possibility of delay found in Jesus' teaching and other early Christian writers (see 1–2 Thessalonians). It clearly announces that the contents of the book are to take place "soon" (1:3), and Jesus himself promises that he will come back "soon" (22:7, 12). The time is at hand; it is near (1:3; 22:10). "For him [John], the parousia of Christ and the consummation of the ages are constantly pressing in, and indeed

---

31. Barr, "Waiting for the End That Never Comes," 107.
32. Bauckham, *Theology of the Book of Revelation*, 157.

Revelation

are always 'at hand.'"[33] Therefore, it would be wrong to insist that John predicted that Christ would come back within his (or his readers') lifetime, but then was mistaken. Like other New Testament authors, John is convinced that the end-time salvation has already begun with the first coming of Christ, the Lamb who has come to offer redemption, form a community of kingdom and priests, and to defeat Satan and death. The church already lives in the time of the end. All that awaits is for the final consummation.

The author of Revelation does not insist that Christ must come back in his lifetime, and never does he tell his audience when Christ is coming back. Rather, Christ could very well come back in their lifetime. And perhaps this expectation was fueled by the conditions under the Roman Empire. John's insistence on the "soon" return of Christ is for exhorational purposes. The fact that Christ could come back soon within the lifetime of the hearers creates an urgency for those who are wavering in their faithful witness to Christ. Christ could come back at any time, and therefore the readers must be prepared lest they find themselves on the wrong end of the stick of God's judgment. As Ben Witherington points out, "John is not interested in date-setting, unlike some writers of apocalyptic material, and . . . the hortatory and rhetorical function of the work as a whole points us in this direction."[34] For John, the end must come, and the fact that it *could* come within the lifetime of his hearers means that they must live in a constant state of vigilance and preparedness so as not to be on the wrong side of God's judgment.

However, Revelation's insistence on the soon return of Christ ("I am coming soon") is balanced with an equally strong strand of delay. That there may be a period of delay is clearly suggested by the cry of the martyrs in the sixth seal (6:9–11): "How long, O Lord," followed by a response that calls for patience in light of the fact that there is a predetermined number of martyrs still to join them. Delay is also built into the very literary structure of Revelation that keeps pushing the end just beyond the reach of the readers, with

33. Smalley, *Revelation to John*, 570.
34. Witherington III, *Revelation*, 280.

stop, starts, interludes, progress, and delay. The literary delay corresponds to a theological tension between imminency and delay. Yet the end will indeed come (21:1—22:5)!

The fact that the church is called upon to finish its faithful witness (Rev 11) suggests a time of delay before the end. Again, in Revelation this has an exhortational function; for the faithful in the church who are suffering persecution and wondering why God has not intervened to bring justice, Revelation provides an answer in the form of the reason for delay—God will indeed vindicate his people, and the end will certainly come, but the church is given time for its faithful witness and the world a chance to repent. Nowhere does John tell us how long the delay will last, but when balanced with the indication of imminence and "soonness," the reader is left with the distinct impression that the end is going to come, but there is no telling when. Revelation entertains the possibility that the end could come within the lifetime of the first readers, or that there could be some delay (without telling us how long of a delay). The two perspectives are held in tension, and the readers are called to live in that tension. "The tension between imminence and delay is heightened, not resolved by the visions, and in this tension readers are called to live out their vocation as witnesses."[35] The readers must be prepared for either scenario by holding on to their faithful witness to Christ no matter what consequences it brings.

---

35. Koester, *Revelation*, 223.

6

Conclusion

Where Is the Promise of His Coming?

The purpose of this final chapter is to reflect both theologically and pastorally on the problem of the delay of the parousia in light of the previous exegetical treatment of the most important passages in the New Testament that touch on this issue. Although these two perspectives cannot be completely separated (theological and pastoral), the first section of this chapter will consider very briefly just a couple of the most important theological implications of the detailed study of the New Testament texts. The second section, then, will consider some of the pastoral implications of the previous chapters.

THEOLOGICAL IMPLICATIONS

Two important theological implications raised by this study that I would like to address are the trustworthiness of Scripture and the sovereignty of God. To put these implications in question form: What bearing does our study of the delay of Christ's coming have on the trustworthiness and the authority of Scripture, and what bearing does it have on our understanding of the sovereignty of God? If the New Testament teaches that Jesus could come back within the lifetime of its first readers, and he did not, what does that say about the trustworthiness of Jesus' teaching, as well as the teaching of his apostles? And if Jesus' coming is imminent but also still subject to possible delay, how does this fit into an understanding of God's sovereignty and the fact that he knows all things? How can God be completely sovereign if the time of his coming is not fixed, but imminent and subject to delay at the same time?

The trustworthiness of Scripture

As we have been reminded throughout this book, it is common for many interpreters of the Bible to see Jesus and his apostles as predicting the coming kingdom and parousia of Christ within the apostles' lifetime, which then never transpired. A possible implication to be drawn from this is that Jesus and his followers were wrong! This is the conclusion of many critical approaches to the texts that we examined above and to this issue in general. If this is the case, what does it say about the trustworthiness of Jesus' and his apostles' teachings? Also by implication, what does this say about the trustworthiness of the New Testament authors more generally and the Scriptures that they have written? My intention is not to mount a full-blown apologetic for the reliability of the New Testament, as this has been done elsewhere, but only to consider the bearing of the topic of the delay of the parousia on how we view Scripture.[1] If Jesus and his followers did indeed predict the coming of Christ and his kingdom in their lifetime, but were then mistaken, this certainly would have a significant effect on how we view a large segment of Jesus' (and the apostles') teaching. Furthermore, if Jesus predicted his second coming and was wrong, then this has implications for our Christology. Jesus would no longer be the perfect Son of God, and the blameless sacrifice for sins (Heb 9:14). Even though Jesus was fully human, this does not entail the likelihood or necessity of error. It is one thing to say that Jesus was ignorant of the timing of his coming (Matt 24:36). It

---

1. For an example see Blomberg, *Can We Still Believe the Bible?*

Conclusion

is quite another thing to say that Jesus predicted wrongly the time of his coming.

We have seen that the burden of Jesus' preaching early on was the nearness of the kingdom of God (Mark 1:3). The coming kingdom and the parousia, which will usher it in, are also an important part of the teaching of Paul and the other apostles. In their writings, the emphasis on nearness of the kingdom frequently functions as a motivation for godly ethical behavior, as well as a key element of the hope of Christians for their vindication in the midst of the harsh realities of this life. Whether one should follow the "slippery slope" argument or not, that if Jesus and his followers were wrong in this area how can we trust them in all other areas, at the very least if Jesus and his followers did get it wrong it calls into question a large swathe of the New Testament teaching. But anecdotally, I have known Christians and students for whom this discrepancy was just too much to bear, leading them to have a "crisis of faith" and even to denounce Christianity altogether and the Scripture on which it is based as untrustworthy. Living nearly two thousand years after the writing of the New Testament, one could question whether our hope is indeed misplaced; two thousand years seems like too long to wait for a return of Christ that was broadcasted in the first century as "near" or "soon." Therefore, if Jesus and his followers were wrong on this, we have reason to question a large segment of their teaching that depends on the soon return of Christ, and perhaps then even reason to raise further doubts about the authority of Scripture as a whole and Christianity and the hope on which it is based.

One of the purposes of this study has been to show that going down this path is unnecessary and unfounded. The above detailed examination of the most relevant New Testament texts has tried to demonstrate two notions: (1) Some of the passages that could be taken as referring to the second coming of Christ at the end of history should not be taken that way. For example, in all three of the Gospels Jesus teaches that the kingdom of God is near or at hand. But was Jesus referring to the final appearance of the kingdom in all its glory at his second coming, or was he referring to the initial but partial, inaugurated form of the kingdom that did indeed come with Jesus' ministry, especially his acts of healing and casting out demons? We argued that the latter is the correct way to understand those passages where Jesus offers entrance into his kingdom immediately for his first listeners.

In a text like Matthew 16:28, it is hard to get around the fact that Jesus is promising that some of his disciples who are standing with him will see Christ come in his kingly power and glory. But does this mean that he was saying that they would be alive to see the second coming at the end of history? In our treatment of that text, I argued that Jesus is most likely not referring to his second coming. Instead, there are a number of more likely options regarding the meaning of Jesus' "coming" in that passage that would have been witnessed by at least some of those standing in Jesus' midst. We argued for a reference to the transfiguration, which is the very next recorded event in all three Synoptic Gospels. Therefore, many texts simply do not refer to the final coming of the kingdom or the second coming of Christ at the end of history, and so cannot be used to cast doubt on Jesus' teaching.

(2) However, other texts do refer to the end-time kingdom and second coming of Christ, and it is said to be "near" or "soon" or "at the door" (e.g., Jas 5:8; 1 Pet 5:7; Rev 22:20). The above chapters have attempted to demonstrate two things about those texts. First, this hope of the soon return of Christ was part and parcel of the early Christian teaching. They always lived with the belief that Christ *could* come back in their lifetime, and therefore it was soon or near. However, these texts fall far short of the authors actually predicting that Christ indeed *will* or *must* come back within their lifetime. Since the end times were already inaugurated with the first coming of Christ, Christians were (and are) already living in the end times, not waiting for the end to come. If they are already in the end, the consummation brought about by the second coming of Christ could come at any time. Time has been compressed, or shortened. *Jesus and other New Testament authors use this perspective as an ethical motivation to holy living, not to predict the end of the world* (in which case they would have been wrong!). If

Conclusion

Christians already live in the end times, there is an urgency since the end times could be brought to a conclusion at any moment with the second coming of Christ. That is, when New Testament authors emphasize the soon return of Christ it is always for ethical motivation, not to predict that Christ will come back in their lifetime, like many of our modern-day soothsayers.

Second, the strong hope in the imminent return of Christ is balanced throughout the New Testament by a note of delay. Texts such as the so-called "Great Commission" in Matthew 28:18–20, as well as the plan of Acts (1:8) for Jesus' followers to be his witnesses to the "ends of the earth," both seem to assume a period of time (without indicating how long) for this to happen. The book of Revelation also sees the church as carrying on its faithful witness to bring about repentance. In at least one of his parables Jesus makes room for delay (Matt 25:1–12), again without hinting at how long this delay might last. Second Peter 3:9–10 offers the most detailed and direct treatment of the problem of the delay of the parousia. God sees things from the perspective of one who is eternal, so that a delay of a thousand years is not significant, as it is for human beings, who see things from the limited perspective of their short lifespan. Furthermore, for Peter, delay simply means more opportunity for humanity to repent. Paul himself thinks there could very well be some delay, since there are certain things that have not happened yet that must happen before the day of the Lord arrives (2 Thess 2:1–12). The book of Revelation also raises the issue of delay in the cry of the martyrs, "how long?" (6:9–11), and the book's very structure has delay (the end never quite gets here!) built into it. So it would be wrong to seize only on the texts that express a soon or imminent return of Christ without giving equal attention to texts that entertain the possibility of some delay, however long that might be.

Perhaps one way to understand the relationship of these two perspectives is through a visual representation.[2] We often think of the biblical view of parousia in light of time running temporally

---

2. I have borrowed this illustration from the commentary by I. Howard Marshall (*Epistles of John*, 149–50).

and directionally in a straight line toward the coming of Christ and the end.

———————————→ The Coming of Christ

The language of "nearness" in the New Testament would seem to suggest that the first readers, or even we, are towards the end of that line. But does time "slow down" as it gets closer to the end and Christ has not come back yet? Or does the line keep getting extended and the end pushed forward as generation follows generation and Christ does not come back? However, this visual illustration needs to be modified in light of the fact that with Christ's first coming he has already inaugurated the end. The church lives in the end times *right now*, a time bounded by the first and second coming of Christ. One way to conceptualize this is by seeing the line as making a bend with the first coming of Christ and running at an angle with the end of all things (the second coming of Christ). The course of time has changed, and it does not run towards the end, but along it and at its brink. It could be visualized like this:

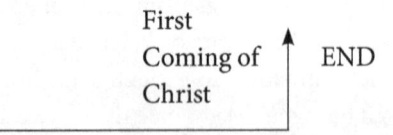

```
       First
       Coming of    ↑    END
       Christ
    _____|
```

Seen in this way, *the end is always near;* time runs along the brink of the end and could "turn" into the end at any time. But the fact that it runs along it means that it could also be delayed, while still being at the brink of and within reach of the end. This helps explain the tension between the imminence or the nearness of the end, and the possibility of delay. Christ could come back at any time, and as those who live close to the end, there is an urgency, without knowing how long time will run alongside the end before it makes the final turn that will conclude the end times (the second coming). The church is called to live within this tension.

When understood in this way (as I think it should be), there is no reason to doubt this part of Jesus' and the apostles' teaching,

Conclusion

and by implication Christianity and the teaching of Scripture overall on which it is based. Instead, we can maintain our confidence in the hope of the coming of Christ and orient our lives towards the Scriptures that testify to that hope. Furthermore, rather than worrying about when the end will come or why it has been delayed, the nearness of the end (as understood above) should motivate us as the people of God to urgency in our mission or faithfully living out and witnessing the gospel in our world. While there is still delay, the church should use this opportunity to fulfill its mission while there is still time.[3]

The sovereignty of God

But this just raises another question: How can God be sovereign over history if the second coming could be soon, or it could be delayed? How does his sovereignty square with Christians' ability to hasten the coming of the Lord (2 Pet 3:12)? Does not God know all things and the beginning from the end? Does not the Father possess exclusive knowledge of when the Son of Man will return (Mark 13:32; Matt 24:36)? Is this not sleight of hand then to say that Christ could come back soon, or that he could delay, and even that we can hasten the coming of Christ, when all along God knows exactly when he will bring history to a close? Or should we see the promises of Christ's coming as more conditional, dependent on human response, so that God "changes his mind" or "resets the date" (maybe even more than once!) in response to the condition of things on this earth?[4]

Again, this is not the place to launch into a detailed discussion on the eternity of God, or the philosophical relationship between divine sovereignty and human responsibility, or the ontological relationship between God and time. (Does God see and experience time the same way we do? Or is God "beyond" and "outside

---

3. This does not mean that the second coming is contingent on the church to the extent that it will not come at all unless the church performs its mission. At the same time, Peter is convinced that we can "speed its coming."

4. Hays, *When the Son of Man Didn't Come*.

of" time?) But we can make a few brief comments to help sort things out and put them in perspective. First, it is worth noting that the New Testament authors themselves saw no embarrassment in setting alongside of each other texts that express God's sovereignty with texts that express both "soonness" and "delay" or uncertainty as to when Christ will return (see Rev 6:9–11; 22:20). New Testament authors anticipated the soon return of Christ, possibly in their lifetime, but also wrestled with the meaning of delay (1 Pet 4:7 vs. 2 Pet 3:8–9). Yet they did not relinquish confidence in God's sovereignty in the arrival of the parousia. Jesus himself told parables that taught both imminence and delay alongside of a statement of God's exclusive knowledge of the time of the Son of Man's return (Matt 24:45–51; 25:1–13, with 24:36). No one knows the day or the hour of Christ's return. Neither do New Testament authors ever make God completely contingent on the events of history or on human response (Matt 24:36). Here we meet another tension in Scripture.

Second, I suspect that this issue of the delay of the parousia is related to another one, the theological relationship between God's sovereignty and human responsibility. Again, without launching into a theological and philosophical reflection, it is best to see the two as standing in some sort of "tension" in the Bible. Some might want to call it a "mystery." Simply put, the New Testament authors are convinced that God is completely sovereign and is not dependent on human response or decisions. Yet at the same time, human beings are responsible agents and God in his sovereignty interacts with and responds to humanity and its decisions.[5] God's sovereignty does not mitigate the genuine choice and response of human beings, yet humanity's actions in no way make God contingent upon them (see Phil 2:12–13). In his sovereignty God takes into account human response and choice. As this tension relates to the coming of Christ, God in his sovereignty knows the time of the second coming of Christ. Yet in his sovereignty he takes into account and chooses to interact with the choices and response of people. Thus, God's people can hasten the coming of Christ (2 Pet

---

5. See Carson, *How Long O Lord?* 177–203.

Conclusion

3:12). Christ might return soon, even within the lifetime of the first-century believers, or there might be delay, for example, to give humanity an opportunity to repent (2 Pet 3:9) and for the gospel to reach the ends of the earth (Acts 1:8; Matt 24:14). Both poles, God's sovereignty and human responsibility, stand alongside each other in the New Testament and need to be retained and emphasized. It is probably beyond our finite comprehension to understand how the two relate, or how all the pieces of the puzzle should be put together, and so we must be content with a certain amount of mystery. Such is the tension between God's sovereignty and human responsibility.

It might be more helpful to think in terms of how these poles of the tension function in the New Testament. God's sovereignty in knowing the time of the end serves to assure God's people that Christ will indeed return to set things right and bring history to its intended goal. Nothing and no one can frustrate God's sovereign purposes. He will indeed bring them to pass, and that is the hope of God's people (Titus 2:13). The coming of Christ is not completely contingent on human affairs. On the other hand, the uncertainty of Christ's return, the fact that it could be soon or there could be a delay, functions to remind us of the need for appropriate human response. The uncertainty serves an exhortational purpose of motivating God's people both to holy living and to faithful witness. If we knew that Christ was going to come back in exactly ten years, we would no doubt arrange our lives in a way to be ready for that time! For most Christians that would mean life as usual up until the end, with time to get things in order right before Christ comes back. Or if we knew for certain that Christ was coming back in twenty-four hours, we would take drastic measures to get things in order immediately and before that time. However, lack of certainty carries with it the need for responsible living at *all* times, since we don't know whether Christ will come back soon or whether there might be some delay. We cannot live as if Christ won't come in our lifetime, nor that he necessarily will. Both sides of the tension are necessary, and serve complimentary (not contradictory) purposes in the New Testament.

PASTORAL IMPLICATIONS

Thinking about the issue of the delay of the parousia, however, is not just a theoretical or merely theological exercise. How we think about the second coming of Christ has profound pastoral implications, some of which have been hinted at throughout this book already but will be unpacked in a little more detail here. The second coming of Christ at the end of history is nothing, if it is not pastorally relevant.

Confidence in Jesus' teaching and Scripture

As I have mentioned elsewhere, the issue of the delay of the coming of Christ is one that often causes Christians to have a crisis of faith and doubt the validity of Christianity and the authority of Jesus and Scripture upon which it is based. How can we trust the Bible, particularly the teachings of Jesus and other New Testament authors, when they seemed to teach that Jesus was going to come back immediately, but he did not? Was Jesus wrong when he taught that he would appear after certain events transpired in the lifetime of his disciples? Did Paul misspeak when he said that the time is short (1 Cor 7:29) or seemed to think that he would be alive at the parousia of Christ (1 Thess 4:13–18)? Was Peter wrong when he taught that the end of all things is near (1 Pet 4:7)? Or what about John in Revelation, who promised that Christ's coming would be soon (22:20)? And if they were wrong on this point, on what other points may they have gotten it wrong? I have known Christians who have abandoned their confidence in Scripture, and even their Christian faith altogether, due to their inability to reconcile such statements with the fact that two thousand years later we still have not witnessed the return of Christ. But one of the implications of this study is that the biblical texts that promise the soon return of Christ can (should?) be understood in a way that does not call into question the veracity of Jesus' and the other apostles' teaching and their writings; they were not predicting the end or concerned with a time scale. They were convinced that they were already living

Conclusion

in the end times; the end had already pressed in upon them, and now they see time in a new light. Christ could come at any time to bring the end times to their consummation. The New Testament itself calls God's people to live within this tension of imminence and delay. Therefore, God's people can have confidence in the Scriptures' testimony to the certainty of the coming of Christ, and therefore we can orient our lives towards the coming of Christ to bring about his promises and vindicate his people. Therefore, there is reason to maintain confidence in Scripture as a whole. A proper perspective on the coming of Christ does not solve all the problems of Scripture, but it does remove a significant barrier to the Scripture's trustworthiness.

Avoiding all "date-setting"

The issue of the delay of the parousia also has much to say to our modern-day infatuation with date-setting and predictions, inspired by current events, of the supposed nearness of Christ's return. Church history is littered with attempts (all failed as of this date!) to calculate the precise date of Christ's return, or more generally to determine whether *we* are the "final generation" who are living in the "last days." In my own lifetime, I remember as a student in grade school sitting in my church and listening to speaker after speaker suggest that due to certain current events (the rise of Russia, the growth of technology, the increase in famines and earthquakes, threats of nuclear war, the appearance of 666 in barcode numbers, etc.), Christ would come back sometime in the next ten or twenty years (that was over forty years ago!). I remember as a seminary student walking out the door of my seminary apartment one morning on the way to class to find a pamphlet left at my front door entitled "88 Reasons Why Christ Will Return in 1988." The author gave a specific date in September based on fantastic calculations and treatments of biblical texts. When Christ did not return on the date specified, the author of the pamphlet admitted to miscalculating and suggested a later date (which also turned out to be wrong!).

Where Is the Promise of His Coming?

Furthermore, I remember while pastoring a church in Montana in the early 1990s during the first Gulf War crisis in Iraq listening to a Christian radio broadcast while driving in my car, where a panel of "prophecy experts" (I will withhold the names to protect the guilty!) was discussing the events of the Gulf War in light of biblical prophecy, or more accurately they were discussing biblical prophecy in light of current events, and were convinced the Gulf War would escalate to become the end-time battle of Armageddon in Revelation (see Rev 16:16); the end was indeed near, Christ's coming was right around the corner! One panelist encouraged listeners to evangelize their unsaved friends and family members, which was good advice. But we should be doing that anyway. Another panelist instructed listeners to empty their savings accounts and cash in CDs and invest it in the Lord's work (presumably his ministry!) since we would not be on this earth much longer to enjoy our belongings. Hopefully no one took his pastorally insensitive appeal seriously; I feel sorry for anyone who did! And on and on it goes! Sadly, such calculations and speculations will no doubt continue until Christ comes back, especially with each major technological development, political shift, threat of war, or proliferation of natural disasters (floods, forest fires, famines, volcanos erupting).

More recently, David Meade, a "biblical numerologist," calculated that the end of the world would transpire on April 23, 2018. Meade based this on Revelation 12:1–2 and modern-day phenomenon of the sun, moon, and Jupiter being in alignment. Again, April 23 came and went without seeing the coming of Christ to earth. The point is, church history is awash with failed attempts to calculate the timing of the soon return of Christ.

But thinking soberly about the delay of the parousia has much to say about how we respond to such tendencies. We have repeatedly noted that Jesus and the New Testament authors shared the same perspective—the first coming of Christ inaugurated the end times, so that the first readers were already living in the end times, not waiting for it to come. In addition they were already experiencing catastrophic events in their day. This meant that they did

Conclusion

not look forward to the end times, but only to *the consummation of the end times in which they were already living*. Therefore, Jesus and the New Testament writers shared the perspective that Christ could come back soon (since they were already in the end). This perspective cannot be missed, and is often set aside or "softened" today in our teaching in reacting against date-setting and false predictions. The fact that church history is littered with examples of false predictions should not blind us to the fact that there is at least a nugget of truth in this approach—Christ *could* come back in our lifetime! When we look out at the world and see threats of war, worsening social or political conditions, and other disasters, we should be reminded that Christ's coming is indeed near. This does not mean that a period of time known as the "end times" is near; we are *already* living in the end times, since the first coming of Christ (see 1 Cor 10:11; Heb 1:2). It also certainly does not mean that we can conclude that Christ's coming will indeed occur within our lifetime, or that such events are unique "signs" pointing to the coming of Christ, or that we are that "last generation" before the end. But neither can we swing the pendulum to the opposite extreme and deny the possibility that Christ could come back and bring things to their conclusion within our lifetime.

Along with the first readers of the New Testament, we too are already living in the end times that have been inaugurated by Christ at his first coming. But the conclusion of the end times with the parousia of Christ could occur at any moment. It is probably impossible to completely recapture the sense of imminency that the early Christians lived with, who first heard the message of the coming kingdom and the nearness of Christ's return. A delay of two thousand years has probably changed the way we read the message of the "soon" return of Christ. Yet at the same time it is all the more necessary for Christians living two thousand years later who are now accustomed to delay to be confronted with the reality that Christ's coming is indeed near. We have grown accustomed to delay and not to see the urgency that the nearness of the return of Christ brought to the first readers. The end is still pressing in on us. The church today needs to attempt to recapture the message of "nearness" or "soon" that provided a powerful motivation and eschatological urgency for the church to pursue holy and godly lives and to fulfill their vocation as faithful witnesses in the world.

The problem is when we seize on this valid perspective (that Christ's coming is near and might occur in our lifetime) but use it to demand that Christ *must* come back soon or that we *must* be that last generation. Often this is accompanied by pointing to different "signs of the times" that herald the end (nuclear war, natural disasters, events in the Middle East, computer chips, etc.), signs that are unique to our generation (every century has claimed unique signs that have never occurred before!). Jesus (Matt 24) as well as John (Rev 6) describe "signs" (wars, rumors of wars, earthquakes, famine) that will take place before the second coming of Christ.[6] However, Jesus makes it clear that these signs do not guarantee that the end is near. They must take place, but they are not the end, and we are not to be deceived by those who would announce the imminent return of Christ based on such signs. Therefore, it is misguided to point to so-called "signs" happening today, such as war, natural disasters, or technological developments, as an indication that the end must occur in our lifetime. Such phenomena are only signposts that point us to the future coming of Christ, not guarantees that Christ is coming back immediately. Such things have occurred (and will continue to occur) throughout history and are not meant to enable us to plot our existence in relationship to the end. They can only remind us that Christ could return at any moment to bring history to its culmination, not that he necessarily will in our lifetime.

What is needed with our infatuation with date-setting and determining the nearness of Christ's coming is the other side of the coin—the New Testament emphasis on possible delay. Those throughout church history who engaged in date-setting and speculation about how near Christ's return is (sometimes with drastic consequences; recall David Koresh and the events in Waco, TX in April 1993, or the person who took out a huge loan thinking that they would not have to pay it back), would have done well

---

6. Schnabel, *40 Questions about the End Times*, 258.

Conclusion

to reflect more seriously on the tension found in the New Testament between imminence and delay. The church today needs to be reminded that things could go on for some time, no matter how unlikely that seems to us. Again, the church is called upon to live within this tension between nearness and delay.

Motivation for holy living

Thinking about the coming of Christ should compel us to respond to it in the same way that the authors of the New Testament expected their first readers to respond. That is, the New Testament teaching on the coming of Christ should function for us in the same way as it did for the first audiences. We saw that consistently across the New Testament's teaching on eschatology the biblical authors appealed to the nearness of Christ's return as a motivation for ethical transformation and holy living, not as a basis for speculation as to the timing of Christ's return. For example, when looking at Jesus' teaching on his return in Matthew 24–25, it is hardly coincidental that the bulk of Jesus' teaching is in the form of parables that enjoin God's people to responsible living in the present. The fact that Christ could come back at any time functioned as a powerful motivator to urgency in the Christian life. It might be tempting to look at two thousand years of delay (since the writing of the New Testament by its original authors) and be lulled into a false sense of security that we have a long life ahead of us. In a sense, like the readers of 2 Peter, we have become used to delay, or "business as usual." Perhaps then for most of us, more than ever, we need to recapture the sense of urgency of the second coming of Christ. This is by no means to suggest that we revert to date-setting, or trying to figure out how close we are to the end by "reading the signs." Rather, we need to be reminded of the message of the New Testament: Christ is coming soon! That is, he could come back within our lifetime, and lest we think that we have all the time in the world to get our lives in order or that life will go on as usual for a while, we need to be confronted with the reality of the imminence of Christ's return. This calls for urgency in evangelism, holy living, and doing acts of justice and mercy.

This receives even greater urgency from the fact that the end-time kingdom of God has already been inaugurated. God's kingdom would bring and would be characterized by love, holiness, righteousness, peace, justice, and mercy. But if the end has already been inaugurated in advance of its final manifestation, then God's people should already be cultivating these virtues. These characteristics of the kingdom should already be evident in the church and in individual Christians to some degree, in anticipation of their perfect manifestation when God's kingdom comes in fullness and power.

This all means that it is wrong for tele-evangelists, pastors, and other Christian leaders to use the coming of Christ as a manipulative tool, e.g., to boost giving, to increase church sizes, to cause bodily harm, to destroy property, to "scare" someone into a conversion experience. Rather, our appeal to the nearness of the second coming of Christ must be in line with how it functions in the New Testament: as a motivation for godly living here and now and to reflect God's holiness, love, and justice in a world that so desperately needs to see it. In other words, a focus on the nearness of the coming of Christ turns our vision back onto our world and the issues that confront us. If Christ is coming soon to set up his kingdom and rule over a new creation (Rev 21–22), then as a people who are already a kingdom of priests (Rev 1:6) and who are already citizens of God's kingdom, we should model and proclaim the gospel and the values of the kingdom and the life of the new creation here and now, in advance of its final and perfect manifestation. We may be the only glimpse of heaven that some people will ever see.

Bibliography

Allen, David. *Hebrews*. New American Commentary. Nashville: Broadman and Holman, 2010.

Allison, Dale. *Jesus of Nazareth: Millenarian Prophet*. Minneapolis: Fortress, 1998.

Aune, David E. *Revelation 17–22*. Word Biblical Commentary. Nashville: Thomas Nelson, 1998.

Barr, David L. "Waiting for the End That Never Comes: The Narrative Logic of John's Story." In *Studies in the Book of Revelation*, edited by Steven Moyise, 101–12. Edinburgh: T. & T. Clark, 2001.

Bateman IV, Herbert W., ed. *Three Central Issues in Contemporary Dispensationalism: A Comparison of Traditional and Progressive Views*. Grand Rapids: Kregel, 1999.

Bauckham, Richard J. *The Climax of Prophecy: Studies on the Book of Revelation*. Edinburgh: T. & T. Clark, 1993.

———. *The Jewish World around the New Testament*. Grand Rapids: Baker, 2008.

———. *Jude, 2 Peter*. Word Biblical Commentary. Waco, TX: Word, 1983.

———. *The Theology of the Book of Revelation*. Cambridge: Cambridge University Press, 1993.

Bauer, W., F. W. Danker, W. F. Arndt, R. W. Gingrich. *A Greek-English Lexicon of the New Testament and Other Early Christian Literature*. 3rd ed. Chicago: University of Chicago Press, 2000.

Beale, Gregory K. *1–2 Thessalonians*. The IVP New Testament Commentary Series. Downers Grove, IL: IVP, 2003.

———. *Revelation*. New International Greek Testament Commentary. Grand Rapids: Eerdmans, 1999.

Bird, Michael F. *Romans*. The Story of God Bible Commentary. Grand Rapids: Zondervan, 2016.

Blomberg, Craig L. *1 Corinthians*. NIV Application Commentary. Grand Rapids: Zondervan, 1994.

———. *Can We Still Believe the Bible?* Grand Rapids: Brazos, 2014.

———. *From Pentecost to Patmos*. Nashville: Broadman and Holman, 2006.

Bibliography

———. *Jesus and the Gospels: An Introduction and Survey.* 2nd ed. Nashville: Broadman and Holman, 2009.

———. *Matthew.* New American Commentary. Nashville: Broadman, 1992.

———. "The Posttribulationalsim of the New Testament: Leaving 'Left Behind' Behind." In *A Case for Historic Premillennialism: An Alternative to "Left Behind" Eschatology*, edited by Craig L. Blomberg and Sung Wook Chung, 61–87. Grand Rapids: Baker, 2009.

Blomberg, Craig L., and Mariam J. Kamell. *James.* Zondervan Exegetical Commentary on the New Testament. Grand Rapids: Zondervan, 2008.

Bock, Darrell L. *Luke 1:1—9:50.* Baker Exegetical Commentary on the New Testament. Grand Rapids: Baker, 1994.

Bock, Darrell L., and Craig A. Blaising. *Progressive Dispensationalism.* Wheaton, IL: Victor, 1993.

Brower, Kent. "Mark 9:1: Seeing the Kingdom in Power." *Journal for the Study of the New Testament* 6 (1980) 17–41.

Bruce, F. F. *1 & 2 Thessalonians.* Word Biblical Commentary. Waco, TX: Word, 1982.

———. *The Epistle to the Hebrews.* New International Commentary on the New Testament. Grand Rapids: Eerdmans, 1964.

Carson, D. A. *The Gospel according to John.* Grand Rapids: Eerdmans, 1991.

———. *How Long, O Lord? Reflections on Suffering and Evil.* 2nd ed. Grand Rapids: Baker, 2006.

———. "Matthew." In *The Expositor's Bible Commentary*, Vol. 9, 25–670. Rev. ed. Grand Rapids: Zondervan, 2010.

Chilton, David. *The Days of Vengeance: An Exposition of the Book of Revelation.* Horn Lake, MS: Dominion, 2006.

Ciampa, Roy, and Brian S. Rosner. *The First Letter to the Corinthians.* Grand Rapids: Eerdmans, 2010.

Cockerill, Gareth Lee. *The Epistle to the Hebrews.* New International Commentary on the New Testament. Grand Rapids: Eerdmans, 2012.

Davids, Peter H. *Commentary on James.* New International Greek Testament Commentary. Grand Rapids: Eerdmans, 1982.

———. *The First Epistle of Peter.* New International Commentary on the New Testament. Grand Rapids: Eerdmans, 1990.

———. *The Letters of 2 Peter and Jude.* Grand Rapids: Eerdmans, 2006.

Davies, W. D., and Dale C. Allison. *Matthew VIII–XVIII.* Vol. II. International Critical Commentary. Edinburgh: T. & T. Clark, 1991.

DeSilva, David. *Perseverance in Gratitude: A Socio-Rhetorical Commentary on the Epistles "to the Hebrews."* Grand Rapids: Eerdmans, 2000.

Ehrman, Bart. *Jesus: Apocalyptic Prophet of the New Millennium.* Oxford: Oxford University Press, 1999.

Fee, Gordon D. *The First Epistle to the Corinthians.* New International Commentary on the New Testament. Rev. ed. Grand Rapids: Eerdmans, 2014.

Bibliography

———. *The First and Second Letters to the Thessalonians*. Grand Rapids: Eerdmans, 2009.
France, Richard T. *The Gospel of Mark*. New International Greek Testament Commentary. Grand Rapids: Eerdmans, 2002.
———. *The Gospel of Matthew*. New International Commentary on the New Testament. Grand Rapids: Eerdmans, 2007.
Garland, David E. *1 Corinthians*. Baker Exegetical Commentary on the New Testament. Grand Rapids: Baker, 2003.
Gentry, Kenneth L. Jr. "A Preterist View of Revelation." In *Four Views on the Book of Revelation*, edited by C. Marvin Pate, 37–92. Grand Rapids: Zondervan, 1998.
Green, Gene. *The Letters to the Thessalonians*. Grand Rapids: Eerdmans, 2002.
———. *Jude & 2 Peter*. Baker Exegetical Commentary on the New Testament. Grand Rapids: Baker, 2008.
Gundry, Robert H. *Matthew: A Commentary on His Handbook for a Mixed Church under Persecution*. 2nd ed. Grand Rapids: Eerdmans, 1994.
Hagner, Donald. *Matthew 14–28*. Word Biblical Commentary. Nashville: Thomas Nelson: 1995.
Hays, Christopher M., et al. *When the Son of Man Didn't Come: A Constructive Proposal on the Delay of the Parousia*. Minneapolis: Fortress, 2016.
Holmes, Michael W. *1 & 2 Thessalonians*. The NIV Application Commentary. Grand Rapids: Zondervan, 1998.
Keener, Craig S. *Acts: An Exegetical Commentary*. Vol 1. Introduction and 1:1–2:47. Grand Rapids: Baker, 2012.
———. *A Commentary on the Gospel of Matthew*. Grand Rapids: Eerdmans, 1999.
Kistemaker, Simon J. *Revelation*. New Testament Commentary. Grand Rapids: Baker, 2001.
Koester, Craig R. *Hebrews*. The Anchor Bible. New Haven: Yale, 2001.
———. *Revelation: A New Translation with Introduction and Commentary*. The Anchor Yale Bible. New Haven: Yale University Press, 2014.
König, Adrio. *The Eclipse of Christ in Eschatology*. Grand Rapids: Eerdmans, 1989.
Kruse, Colin. *Paul's Letter to the Romans*. Grand Rapids: Eerdmans, 2012.
Ladd, George E. *A Theology of the New Testament*. Grand Rapids: Eerdmans, 1974.
Longenecker, Richard H. *The Epistle of Paul to the Romans*. New International Greek Testament Commentary. Grand Rapids: Eerdmans, 2016.
Marshall, I. H. *1 and 2 Thessalonians*. The New Century Bible Commentary. Grand Rapids: Eerdmans, 1983.
———. *Acts*. Tyndale New Testament Commentary. Grand Rapids: Eerdmans, 1980.
———. *The Epistles of John*. New International Commentary on the New Testament. Grand Rapids: Eerdmans, 1978.

Bibliography

Mathewson, Dave. "Revelation in Recent Genre Criticism: Some Implications for Interpretation." *Trinity Journal* 13 (1992) 193–213.

McKnight, Scot. *The Letter of James*. New International Commentary on the New Testament. Grand Rapids: Eerdmans, 2011.

Michaels, J. Ramsey. *1 Peter*. Word Biblical Commentary. Waco, TX: Word, 1988.

Moo, Douglas J. *The Epistle to the Romans*. New International Commentary on the New Testament. Grand Rapids: Eerdmans, 1996.

———. *The Letter of James*. Grand Rapids: Eerdmans, 2000.

Moore, A. L. *The Parousia in the New Testament*. Leiden: Brill, 1966.

Mounce, Robert H. *Revelation*. New International Commentary on the New Testament. Grand Rapids: Eerdmans, 1977.

Osborne, Grant R. *Matthew*. Zondervan Exegetical Commentary on the New Testament. Grand Rapids: Zondervan, 2010.

———. *Revelation*. Baker Exegetical Commentary on the New Testament. Grand Rapids: Baker, 2002.

Pao, David W. *Acts and the Isaianic New Exodus*. 2000. Reprint. Grand Rapids: Baker, 2002.

Pate, C. Marvin. *The Glory of Adam and the Afflictions of the Righteous*. New York: Edwin Mellen, 1993.

Perriman, Andrew. *The Coming of the Son of Man: New Testament Eschatology for an Emerging Church*. Milton Keynes, UK: Paternoster, 2005.

Plevnik, Joseph. *Paul and the Parousia*. Peabody, MA: Hendrickson, 1997.

Schnabel, Eckhard. *40 Questions about the End Times*. Grand Rapids: Kregel, 2011.

Schreiner, Thomas R. *1, 2 Peter, Jude*. New American Commentary. Nashville: Broadman and Holman, 2003.

Schweitzer, Albert. *The Quest for the Historical Jesus: A Critical Study of Its Progress from Reimarus to Wrede*. Translated by W. Montgomery. London: Black, 1910.

Smalley, Stephen S. *The Revelation to John: A Commentary on the Greek Text of the Apocalypse*. Downers Grove, IL: IVP, 2005.

Thiselton, Anthony. *The First Epistle to the Corinthians*. New International Greek Testament Commentary. Grand Rapids: Eerdmans, 2000.

Turner, David L. *Matthew: Baker Exegetical Commentary on the New Testament*. Grand Rapids: Baker, 2008.

Walvoord, John F. *The Revelation of Jesus Christ*. Chicago: Moody, 1966.

Winter, Bruce W. "Secular and Christian Responses to Corinthian Famines." *Tyndale Bulletin* 40 (1989) 86–106.

Witherington III, Ben. *Jesus, Paul and the End of the World: A Comparative Study of New Testament Eschatology*. Downers Grove, IL: IVP, 1992.

———. *Paul's Letter to the Romans: A Socio-Rhetorical Commentary*. Grand Rapids: Eerdmans, 2004.

Wright, N. T. *Jesus and the Victory of God*. London: SPCK, 1996.

Scripture Index

EXTRA-BIBLICAL LITERATURE

2 Baruch
23:4–5	90

2 Clement
12:6	66

1 Enoch
47:1–4	90
93:9	55

4 Ezra
4:35–37	90

b. Sanhedrin
98a	66

Sirach
36:7	66

b. Yoma
86b	66

OLD TESTAMENT

Exodus
23:16	21
34:6	64
34:22	21

Leviticus
23:42–43	21

Deuteronomy
18:15–19	20

Psalms
6:3	90
13:1–2	90
74:10	90
79:5	90
80:4	90
89:46	90
90:4	63
90:13	90
94:3	90

Isaiah
44:3	39
49:6	40n4, 41
59:21	39
60	14
60:12	14
60:22	66
65:17–25	14

Scripture Index

Jeremiah

12:4	90
29:10–14	10

Ezekiel

34–37	8, 14
36:26–27	39
37:14	39
40:2	21

Daniel

7	28
7:9	20
7:13	21
9:1–27	10
10:5–6	20
10:13	57
10:20–21	57
11:30–45	56
12:1	57

Joel

1–2	28
2	19
2:11	54
2:28	39

Micah

4:5	20

Habakkuk

1:2	90

Zephaniah

1:7	54

Zechariah

14	14
14:1	54
14:16–21	21

NEW TESTAMENT

Matthew

3:17	13
4:17	2, 15
4:23	16
6:10	16, 66
10:1—11:1	22
10:1–16	23
10:5–15	23
10:17–42	23, 24, 25
10:17	23
10:18–19	24
10:18	23
10:22	24, 25
10:23	22, 23, 24, 25
11:2–5	16
12:28	16
13	16
16:21–26	18
16:28	3, 17, 19, 36, 100
17:1–13	19
17:1	20
17:2	21
17:5	21
24–25	3, 19, 26, 29, 30, 33, 111
24	7, 33, 69, 110
24:4–28	33
24:6–26	29
24:8	33
24:9	33
24:10–12	55
24:14	36, 105
24:15–28	32
24:15–22	28, 29, 32, 33
24:21	32
24:22	32
24:24	55
24:29–32	28, 29
24:29–31	27, 28
24:29	26, 31, 32, 33
24:33	29, 70, 81
24:34	3, 26, 28, 29, 31
24:36	30, 36, 39, 98, 103, 104
24:43	84

Scripture Index

24:44	81	24:49	39
24:45–51	30, 31, 33, 36, 104		

John

24:48	30
24:50	30
25:1–13	30, 31, 33, 36, 101, 104
25:5	30
25:31–46	16, 37, 69
28:18–20	24, 25, 36, 41, 101
28:20	25

21	34
21:19	34, 35
21:20–21	34
21:22–23	3
21:22	34, 35
21:23	34, 35

Mark

Acts

1:3	99
1:15	2, 13, 15, 16
8:31–38	18
9:1	3, 17, 19, 36
9:2–13	19
9:2	20
13	3, 7, 19, 26, 33
13:4	29
13:7–23	29
13:14–20	28, 29
13:23–27	27, 28, 29
13:24–25	7
13:24	26, 31
13:29	29, 81
13:30	3, 26, 27, 28, 29
13:32	30, 36, 103
13:33	81

1	40, 41
1:5	39
1:7	40
1:8	39, 40, 60, 101, 105
1:9	38
1:10	40
1:11	41
2	19, 39
2:17–21	19
2:31–36	19
28	39

Romans

9:6	4
13–14	42
13	42
13:11	42
13:12	42
13:1–10	42
13:11–14	42, 68
13:14	42

Luke

1 Corinthians

4:43	2, 13, 15
9:21–26	18
9:27	3, 17, 18, 19, 36
9:28–36	19
9:28	20
12:39	84
21	3, 7, 27, 33
21:9–21	29
21:20–24	28, 29
21:25–28	27, 28, 29
21:25	26, 31
21:28	29
21:31	3
21:32	26, 28, 29

6:14	52
7:25–32	44
7:25–32	47n24
7:25	60
7:26	44, 45
7:27–31	45
7:28	46
7:29	3, 44, 45, 46, 71, 81, 106
7:31	44, 48
10:11	48, 109

119

Scripture Index

1 Corinthians (continued)
15:52 — 9

2 Corinthians
1:4–7 — 46
4:14 — 52
5:1 — 52

Ephesians
1:19–22 — 19

Philippians
1:20–24 — 52
1:29–30 — 46
2:12–13 — 104

1 Thessalonians
4–5 — 55
4:13—5:11 — 49, 50
4:13–18 — 9, 51, 106
4:15–17 — 3
4:15 — 51, 52
4:17 — 51
5 — 59
5:1 — 53
5:2–6 — 54
5:2–4 — 84, 85
5:10 — 52

2 Thessalonians
2 — 58, 60
2:1–12 — 53, 54, 55, 58, 101
2:1b-2 — 54
2:3 — 55, 56
2:4 — 56, 57
2:5–7 — 57
2:5 — 56, 57
2:6–7 — 56
2:6 — 56, 57
2:7 — 56, 58
2:8 — 56
2:9–11 — 56
2:12 — 56

1 Timothy
4:1 — 55

Titus
2:13 — 105

Hebrews
1:2 — 68, 72, 73, 109
9:14 — 98
10:25 — 3, 67, 68, 81

James
5:1–11 — 68
5:7–8 — 68
5:7 — 69
5:8 — 3, 6, 69, 71, 81, 100
5:9 — 69

1 Peter
4:7 — 3, 6, 9, 70, 100, 104, 106

2 Peter
2:1–3 — 62
2:11–16 — 62
3 — 61, 62, 67, 69
3:1–4 — 62
3:3–4 — 10
3:3 — 64
3:4 — 4, 62
3:5–10 — 62
3:5–7 — 63
3:8–12 — 10
3:8–10 — 62, 73
3:8–9 — 63, 64, 104
3:8 — 63
3:9–10 — 101
3:9 — 64, 105
3:10 — 48, 63, 84
3:11–12 — 64
3:11 — 64
3:12 — 63, 64, 65, 66, 103, 104–5
3:13 — 67

Scripture Index

1 John

2:8	72
2:17	48, 71, 72n22
2:18	71, 72, 73

Revelation

1:1–3	77
1:1	3, 74, 79
1:3	3, 74, 79, 80, 94
1:4	80
1:6	77, 112
1:7	21
1:13–16	20
1:18	77
2–3	75, 79, 82
2:5	83
2:10	81
2:16	81, 82
2:25	83, 84, 85
2:27	83
2:27	83
3:3	84
3:11	81, 82, 83
4–5	75
5	91, 93
5:1–2	92
5:5	77
5:9–10	77
6	92, 110
6:9–11	89, 95, 101, 104
6:10	89
6:11	90
6:12–17	92
7	92
8–9	92
8	92
8:1	92
8:2	92
9	92
10–11	93
10:7	93
11	93, 94
11:1–13	93
11:15	93
11:16–18	93
11:19	93
12–14	93
12–13	75, 79, 93
12	93
12:1–2	108
12:4	76
12:7–11	77
12:10	81
12:12	87, 93
13	93
16	93
16:15	84
16:16	108
17–18	94
17	3, 85
17:8–18	85
17:9–11	3, 85
17:9	87
17:10	86
17:11	86, 87
19–22	76, 77
19–20	79
19:11—20:15	94
19:15	82
19:21	82
20:1–15	87
20:1–10	16, 94
20:3	94
20:4–6	9, 83
21–22	112
21:1—22:5	94, 96
21:10	21
22:1–5	83
22:6–21	79
22:6	3
22:7	79, 82, 94
22:10	3, 76, 79, 80, 94
22:12	74, 79, 82, 94
22:20	2, 4, 74, 79, 82, 100, 104, 106